# LETTERS TO BRIAN

## 23 November 2011

Several decades ago, when we were a young and carefree married couple, we were robbed. Painters had come into our apartment and one of them, a profusely perspiring glassy-eyed guy our age, helped himself to Brian's wallet. We didn't realize it had gone missing until later that evening when city police arrived at our door. The thief had tried to buy gas with Brian's credit card, making the fatal mistake of forging his signature: Brain Brooks.

## 10 January 2012

It's been two months less a day since Brian's diagnosis: inoperable glioblastoma. As I write this he is up at the dining room table grumbling about our finances. Over the time when he moved from bouts of crying and wild optimism to a full-blown steroid-induced psychosis that landed him, over Christmas, on the psych ward, we cut up his credit cards. Today we purchased another pair of eyeglasses at Costco—nothing like the round ones he'd wanted over a month ago to make him look like Steve Jobs, and they would have been flattering had we found them, hang the cost. His most recent pair got tossed, inadvertently, into the trash at the hospital sometime over the past three weeks. Everyone there turned the place upside down trying to find them—to no avail.

Today, he is upset, and I don't blame him, to have to spend more money on new glasses. "We're spending money like drunken sailors!" he said.

So we're back to a saner place that includes frugality. But now he doesn't understand why he can't drive the car. When we explain that he has a brain tumour with its accompanying brain injury, he still doesn't get that that's why he shouldn't be behind the wheel. I have stopped driving. Grief and its accompanying trauma are bad seatmates. Someday I'll drive again, but for now I'm a danger to myself and everyone else on the road.

And I have not wanted to write—writing being as natural to a writer as breathing. Through many dark days where two months feels like two years, breathing is all I can do, one breath at a time through an endless series of shocks to the spirit, body and psyche.

In spite of the fact that the tumour is in his speech centre (his difficulty with word finding was the first thing that gave his condition away), he speaks fairly well now and even (very slowly) reads. He was abruptly taken off everything when his mind collapsed, but the radiation in combination with the chemo drugs and the steroids, according to his oncologist, "seem to have kicked the crap out of the tumour," and he's stable. For this miracle I am grateful. We have entered a period of grace, a flow to be regarded with gingerly respect. I am a bright woman. I know there is no road map for this stuff. As a writer I deal with ambiguities. Our life has been torn asunder and glued back together. It looks suspiciously like our old life, but I'd be a fool to think that it is.

## 11 January 2012

I need to pay attention. Enjoy this time. Stop in the middle of it all, take a breath and return to my original thoughts, the state of gratitude and grace that flowed so abundantly from my spirit before all this happened. Last fall—and all through the summer at Eden—the equation of "we," of "us." The bucket list I referred to in the cottage journal: nothing left on it, I claimed, except several more summers at the lake with Brian.

Supper at the Brooks'—tofu, quinoa, stir-fried vegetables, cookies freshly baked. Patricia Barber, jazz artist extraordinaire, playing in the background. "Nobody writes lyrics like her," Brian remarked at the table. Fire going. Cold night outside. Later, we'll slip into bed, listen to each other's breath, look at the shadows on the ceiling, just be—hip-to-hip. I love this man.

# LETTERS TO BRIAN

## A YEAR OF LIVING AND REMEMBRANCE

### BY MARTHA BROOKS

TURNSTONE PRESS

Letters to Brian: A Year of Living and Remembrance
copyright © Martha Brooks 2015

Turnstone Press
Artspace Building
206-100 Arthur Street
Winnipeg, MB
R3B 1H3 Canada
www.TurnstonePress.com

MIX
Paper from
responsible sources
FSC® C016245

All rights reserved. No part of this book may be reproduced or transmitted in any
form or by any means—graphic, electronic or mechanical—without the prior written
permission of the publisher. Any request to photocopy any part of this book shall be
directed in writing to Access Copyright, Toronto.

Turnstone Press gratefully acknowledges the assistance of the Canada Council
for the Arts, the Manitoba Arts Council, the Government of Canada through the
Canada Book Fund, and the Province of Manitoba through the Book Publishing Tax
Credit and the Book Publisher Marketing Assistance Program.

Photo pages ii and 207 by Maureen Brooks.

Printed and bound in Canada by Friesens for Turnstone Press.

Library and Archives Canada Cataloguing in Publication

Brooks, Martha, 1944-, author

    Letters to Brian : a year of living and remembrance / Martha Brooks.

ISBN 978-0-88801-521-1 (pbk.)

    1. Brooks, Martha, 1944- --Marriage. 2. Brooks, Brian, 1943-2012--

Death and burial. 3. Authors, Canadian (English)--20th century--Biography.

4. Grief. 5. Loss (Psychology). I. Title.

PS8553.R663Z47 2015          C818'.5403          C2014-907888-9

*To Brian, of course,*
*for the gifts of your life and your love.*

somehow sweetly alive
these ghosts that i inhale
the moon and i survive
while the dearly dead prevail

"The Wind Song"
—Patricia Barber

# LETTERS TO BRIAN

*. . . contentedly inseparable . . .*

My husband, Brian, about a year before his devastating diagnosis of brain cancer, read aloud to me an excerpt, published in *The Atlantic*, from *A Widow's Story*, a memoir by the American author Joyce Carol Oates. She and her husband Raymond Smith seemed to have been an extraordinarily close couple and, as Brian observed, "They sound like us." We were at the family cottage on Pelican Lake at the time ... contentedly inseparable ... our own long marriage began in 1967. Unaware of what was to come, we had nothing more spectacular on our mutual bucket list than many more summers there, joined at the hip.

Brian's diagnosis came on Remembrance Day, 2011, and through the last year of his life, he and I, together with our daughter, Kirsten, who had just turned thirty-nine, treated his disease not as a death sentence, which it surely was, but as an opportunity to tighten our bond and appreciate whatever time would be given. By the spring of 2012, Brian was well enough to welcome the miracle of another season at the family cottage—our "Eden" place—and that's where he and I spent the next six months.

I kept a journal of the time from when he was first diagnosed, and all through that summer and into the fall—a scattering of entries recording an ever more excruciating awareness of the fragility of his situation. After his death on November 27, 2012, at 9:27 A.M., I found myself turning more and more to its pages for solace and shelter. After all, I was and am a writer, fully equipped to wrap my heart and mind around grief—and to use those words as a way into the hard but necessary work of grieving.

That was all well and good for a while, but a month after his death, I picked up my pen and surprised myself by writing, "My darling Brian." The words that followed flowed into a letter to him. And while, in my sorrow, I realized that my handsome husband would never again appear in the doorway, all six-foot-six of him,

I also realized that he could be a kind of long-distance lover. Here he was, the man of my heart and best friend, with whom I could share thoughts as we had always done. I just never expected to hear back! Yet, and here is the surprising thing, what should have been a one-way communication quickly led to the synchronous and the miraculous in a kind of call-and-response between us that allowed me, ultimately, to cleave to the mortal while still carrying his love around like a lucky charm.

Letters to Brian, the book, concludes at the first anniversary of his death. However, I continue to heal by staying connected to him. I summer in the valley we both loved. And as I write this, mid-August 2014, I still, almost every day, pick up a pen to tell him how much I love him and give him news from home. Not to do so would be to close myself off from the longest and most profound relationship of my life.

# JOURNAL ENTRIES

## 17 January 2012

Brian said to me today, "We've had a pretty good run at it. And we're not done, yet."

## 15 February 2012

I'm now back to driving. Brian and I took a trip out to Ninette and the cottage overlooking a frozen Pelican Lake, yesterday, Valentine's Day, to celebrate just being together—a noble accomplishment. He's been depressed. Well, why wouldn't he be. Actually we both have. But yesterday our country friend, Marilyn, and I were with him in the yard at the cottage as we all noted the sun coming through the branches of the winter trees. Then, when Brian walked a little way into the woods we slowly followed him. So quiet in there. He raised his eyes and just stood there, looking around, before he said, "It's lovely."

## 21 February 2012

"A light has burned out behind my desk in my office—I just noticed it," I say to Brian.

"Okay," he says, lifting his head from the newspaper, "I'll deal with it."

He likely won't but it's good for him to think that he might.

"I just made red lentil soup with fresh tomatoes and roast cumin," I tell him.

"Smells good," says my husband, who for the past decade has done almost all of the cooking.

Now I sit in the living room with him, pen in hand, glass of sherry on the coffee table. Moments of treasured normalcy in the Brooks household. Holding fast this moment, this day, the rustle of the newspaper in his hands. Heartbreaking.

## 6 March 2012

We are taking great pleasure in being together—in the extraordinary ordinariness of it. No drama. The lovely mundane everyday beauty of us.

## 8 March 2012

A sunny afternoon. We're in bed and I start to cry.

"What's wrong?" he says.

"I can't stand the thought of you not being here, of losing you."

He gives me his lovely smile, head turned on the pillow, and says, "That's why I'm not going anywhere. I told you right from the beginning I wasn't."

"That's good," I say. "I'll hold you to it because I'm drowning in my own tears, here—gives a whole new meaning to that."

## 14 March 2012

Today we went to Rona and purchased dime-sized discs for my desk. Back home we lifted each corner of heavy glass and secured all four so that it no longer teeters precariously. A small job (with gratitude from me) that lifted his spirits. Gratitude, that word, again, is immeasurably healing.

Such a strikingly beautiful yet simple desk. He designed it for me with all of his genius intact.

Still is a genius.

## 18 March 2012

A wonderful family Sunday. The best, Kirsten and I agreed, since her dad got sick. Brian was very clear and funny. Dinner, a baked tomato polenta—which he himself has made for years but now claimed he couldn't remember ever having eaten—arrived at the table, fragrant with fontina and gorgonzola and fresh herbs. Despite his memory loss I really think he was having us on. He isn't above doing that. He tucked into it and we had a free and easy time, and Mike had three helpings, egged on by his father-in-law. Later, sitting around the living room, with the screen door to the patio open, in March in Manitoba of all things, we four chatted about everything and nothing as a warm fragrant breeze blew through. Spring and summer all at once. A moment in time.

## 23 April 2012

Twenty degrees. Painted my toenails blossom pink in honour of the season. A continuation of all good things. Bravely forth. May 1st and a summer on the hilltop overlooking Pelican Lake in three of its seasons, with my man, is now in sight.

## 25 April 2012

"Be grateful for luck. Pay the thunder no mind—listen to the birds. And don't hate nobody."—Eubie Blake

## 1 May 2012

At the cottage at last. Frankly, wondered if we'd make it here together this year. But the maniac gulls welcome us and the sun and the pastel blue sky of spring and the fiery green leaves. Home.

## 3 May 2012

Yesterday, while Brian mowed the lawn, Myra and I took a walk through the woods. I picked sunny yellow marsh marigolds from a cold stream and brought them home and put them on the table and then cooked us a blueberry crumble cake and stir-fries. Myra is in a constant state of canine rapture.

## 4 May 2012

We drove in the rain to Belmont. At Dolder's Nursery, with its earth-rich plant smells, we purchased a very large rosemary plant which now resides in the breezeway and smells wonderful. Last year a rosemary I'd planted outside the cottage, under the protection of the French lilac bushes near the front door, did not survive the heat of summer. We always dig up a rosemary and take it back in the fall to our city kitchen window, and when it died that felt somehow like a bad omen. As bad omens go, if you believe that sort of thing, it certainly was one. Anyway, this rosemary, lively and succulent and bushy, practically breathes. Let's see if we can get it and ourselves back to city life, safely, come fall.

## 18 May 2012

I suspect I am, ever so gently, being eased out of the kitchen. Confidence is a great motivator—mine, as well as his. I did say to him, yesterday, "Anytime you're ready to kick me out of here let me know and I'll go gladly." He's still a genius cook—as his improvised tomato-tofu dish, yesterday, attests to—and he was pleased that it was so good. Have I mentioned, lately, here in these pages, how much I love this man? His gentleness, his sanity, his thoughtfulness, his sensible and reasoned approach to life and to me. What a rare bird he is. What a lucky woman I am. Forty-nine years and counting. When you love somebody, when they are the right person for you, there are never enough years.

## 6 June 2012

After much prodding from Brian and a little more from our friend Marilyn, I've jumped back into the writing. Clarity, speed, joy—it's all there—and the novel, at last, is taking shape.

## 1 July 2012

Been working at getting my jazz voice back in shape. I sing all the time, now, to my appreciative husband. It's been a year since the Winnipeg Jazz Festival and I'm a little rusty, but singing is always such a pleasure. Went back to the city to do a gig. Rob Siwik walked into the place to set up his drum kit, said "Hi" to Brian who was, as usual, sitting front and centre, and then he added a completely impromptu, "She's in great voice." Brian beamed and squeezed my hand three times. Then for the next three hours Jeff Presslaff and Rob and my longtime bassist, Steve Hamilton, played sublimely and tenderly and I sang for the folks but mostly for my husband. Our friend Pat, who came out to hear us, said that the music shifted something in her DNA. Brian, hugging me close the next morning, my ear next to his heart, said, "You needed that. You needed it for you."

## 15 July 2012

In Brian's hand, "Hapey Birsthday, Marth (a clump of ink) a. All My Love—Brian"

"I made a mess of it," he said, shaking his head and handing it to me.

"No you didn't," I said, pressing his message to my heart, "it's perfect. I love it."

### 8 August 2012

Been a month of comings and goings and, mostly, stayings. The tumour is growing again and we're trying temozolomide once more. He survived his first week of chemo pills (three weeks off and then another week on). The week after he was tired and unwell. This week, after a two-hour round of reiki with his favourite daughter, he's feeling better.

### 9 September 2012

Golden autumn day. Wind lullaby in the leaves. Kirsten and Mike out for another weekend and she's staying for the week and wants to give her favourite father a few more reiki treatments. Each day in Eden is a blessing. When we arrived in May we couldn't have predicted that we'd still be enjoying a (relatively) normal life, seeing to fruition an entire spring, summer and fall here.

### 15 September 2012

Kirsten's birthday, and the day after we received the remarkable news that after only two rounds of the beautiful chemo drug temozolomide, his tumour has shrunk. This is a rare early response, say his medical team at CancerCare. "He's doing wonderfully well," said his nurse, Pam, who gave us the results of his latest MRI. So he's living with his disease and now there are signs that he may be able to continue to do so. Praise be.

### 2 October 2012

After three dark blue journals I've decided, with this new one, to go with a little colour. Orange suits my present mood, it is Brian's favourite colour, and it's not only a spiritual colour but is autumnal as well as cheerful. Still residing at Pelican Lake, where the colours are gold and orange and life has a larger sense of stretch. Whereas every moment up until recently in this past year was filled with or at least backlit by sorrow and loss, there is room now to breathe and ponder. We don't know what's up ahead, but you live side by side with uncertainty as your travelling companion and make some kind of peace with it or there's no living at all.

## 22 October 2012

Raining, the pastures need greening up. Just finished an entry in the cottage journal, what nephew Brian refers to as "the life of the cottage." So many images of this past summer. If I have to choose one, though, it would be my own Brian and me having meals out on the lower deck—tablecloth, flowers, bistro-style—with that wide wide expanse of landscape, miles of lake with its fringe of hills, and that other mirroring landscape—long pearly clouds set in a very blue summer sky. Seated at the edge of the deck like that, within the tops of trees, it's a floating feeling, truly heavenly. Brian loved the meals there, it really was the high point of his day. I'm so grateful for him and the summer I never thought we'd have in this beautiful beloved place.

## 25 October 2012

This morning I wrote a parting note in the cottage journal. "8:40 A.M.—Built a farewell fire last night. Fires all have personalities. This one went from 4:30 to 9:30, strong and cheerful. Brian remarked, 'It didn't go crazy—just kept on.' Trick, of course, is steady feeding, a log every half hour. We had dinner and then sat all evening to watch the flames, the hot coals, the crackle and snap, the primal beauty of it, as the summer in review slowed and the peace of this place descended. We'll always be here in spirit if not in body. As we closed up for the night I stood in front of the gleaming dancing embers and thanked the fire. Bye for now ..."

*(Author note: between October 25 and the next journal entry there are no other entries.)*

## Last day of November, 2012 – 9:35 P.M.

A peace descends when someone dies. I feel him, warmly, hand still on my back. His wedding ring is on the middle finger of my right hand. But it's unbelievable that he isn't here. And yet every inch of this house carries a memory of him. Every inch of my skin holds the cell memory of his touch. Oh, my darling.

## 8 December 2012

Sorrow. Sorrow. Sorrow.
  Sorrow. Sorrow. Sorrow.

## 9 December 2012

There is really no safe place for me to fall. It's a lonely lonely journey. Can't in all reality be taken by anyone but me. I truly want to die. To die and be with Brian who was my only safe place. Oh God, sorrow, sorrow, sorrow. This world is too much for me. Where is he? I can't find him in my dreams. I can't find him lying beside me. I can't find him, except in passing—a flicker, a gesture—in the people he most loved. I am alone in a crowd. I am alone in the midst of people who love me dearly. People say, "I can't imagine it," and I say, "I'm having trouble even imagining it myself." I hate this life and no longer want it. I only want him.

## 17 December 2012—8:53 P.M.

Went with Kirsten and her old friend, Vincent, to Shelmerdine's today. Purchased fragrant greens for the house. No tree this year. Bought a plush rabbit puppet—very lifelike. Kirsten set him up on the fireplace on the wine velvet bag covering the cardboard box that contains Brian's ashes, which are pale pink. Candles all around. It's all lovely. I'm so sad. I'm writing again. Honouring a wish that Brian had for me. I want to sleep. I want only to dream of him. Of my darling darling man.

# BOOK ONE

# WINTER

"Shit happens—and there you have it."
— Brian Brooks


"Grief is not a state—it's a continent."
— Martha Brooks

## Thursday 27 December 2012

My darling Brian,

One month dead. Forty-nine years sadly behind me. So, on this peculiar anniversary, darling, let me start a conversation with you.

This morning I looked at the room temperature in our bedroom and it read 61 degrees. Came downstairs to discover that the furnace isn't working. After calling the gas company I sat down to have breakfast and discovered that one of my teeth is cracked close to the front of my mouth. Its loss would seriously compromise my smile and (in your own words, "You are beautiful") evidently my beauty. As I sat in the dentist's chair, a lucky break, half an hour later—in the very room where last year you had your tooth fixed and I'd had to translate your faltering speech to the tender young dentist who looked after you—I was attended by his equally tender replacement. When I burst into tears and she said, "Oh I'm so sorry, your tooth must really hurt," I sobbed, "I'm so sorry to carry on like this, my husband just died and the furnace broke down this morning and I noticed, on the way coming over here, that my car is making funny noises."

"Oh, God," she said, "I can help you with your tooth."

As I sat there, I could hear you say, "You have to work with me on this. Do what it takes to fix this tooth properly."

I miss you every day, every hour, every minute. Your favourite broadcaster on CBC, Julie Nesrallah, keeps me company this morning. It's 11:42 A.M.

I feel your gentle nudge, reminding me that I normally spend five hours of every working day inside the altered universe of my writing, that it's always been a kind of home. More then ever these days, it also brings me solace. Do you remember our ongoing daily discussions about the work? Ah, Brian, maybe I'll find you there.

All my love,
Martha

### 28 December 2012

Darling Brian,

Our friends Sharon and Darvin made a mercy run to see me last night—as they have done all through this ordeal. They brought homemade goodies and a shawl they picked up in Arizona. "Just a little something to keep you warm," Sharon said.

I watched these two people fall in love when they were teenagers. Like ourselves, they know the deep comfort of having a partner who understands you. I told them that you were always ready to reach out and put your hand on my back, steadying me when I didn't even know that that was what I needed.

Sharon said, "That should be your mantra, now—let me write it down for you." And then she wrote in this orange journal: "My hand on your back. Stay steady …"

All my love,
Martha

### Sunday, 30 December 2012

Darling Brian,

I am thinking about those famous lines from *Beautiful Losers*. Leonard Cohen's right, God is indeed alive and magic is certainly afoot. That venter motor in the furnace that needed replacing—a young service guy arrives, late in the evening, after making twelve service calls. He's already talked to our Kirsten's Mike, who has been bonding with him on their cels. Last service call, his truck got towed. He should have been in a terrible mood. He walks in and I say, "Did you even have supper, honey?"

"Five o'clock, at McDonald's," he says, and goes straight to work. Pulls out the old motor as I'm hanging around, looks at it and says, "Heck of a thing at Christmas."

I tell him, "Well, it's worse, my husband just died."

He looks at me. "Expensive to replace—about $500."

"I guess so," I say, not sure whether he means the motor or my husband. Then I hear your voice in my head, Brian, and add, "Well, keep it simple."

"So," he goes on, "my boss is a really good guy and he's gone south for Christmas, but this time of year he'll sometimes cut one customer some slack," and off he goes to his truck to get some heaters so we don't freeze overnight. Mike follows him outside to offer a hand.

"Did she really just lose her husband?" the guy asks, like it's a helluva thing that he's just simply trying to get his head around.

"Yeah, she did," Mike concurs. (He tells me this later.)

"Well," he says, "I'll be back bright and early tomorrow morning."

He comes back next day, early like he promised, replaces the motor, and charges me $110.

"My boss likes everything done right," he tells me.

"Sounds like my husband," I say, as I pay him.

He goes back to his truck, gets his card, hands it to me, places his other hand on my shoulder and says, "You're going to be okay."

Next thing I'm off to Sturgeon Creek Garage, serenaded by the high-pitched squeals of the car. I'd phoned ahead to tell them what was wrong. It occurs to me that the owner, Wally, in his white lab coat and with his crazy long white hair, resembles Doc in *Back to the Future*. Anyway, as I'm pulling up, noisily, Wally and his office manager look out their window and wave to me. I come inside and Wally, with his gentlemanly car-side manner, comes up to me, looks me in the eyes, says, "I'm so sorry for your loss." After that he hugs me and then we stand, side by side, looking at the work order for our 2001 Hyundai.

"I don't want to put any more money in it," I say. "I'm finally getting a new one."

"What kind?" he asks, solicitously.

"Toyota," I tell him.

"Not a hybrid," he cautions.

"No," I say, "a Matrix."

"Oh, good," he says, relieved. "You'll have no trouble with that one—it's a very good car."

So, I sit in the sanity of Wally's shop while his mechanics work on our car. They have no apparent rough edges, these men, they are all gentlemen. About an hour later the car is fixed. No more screams and squeals. Wally hands me the bill—$67.

Yes, darling, you are still taking care of me. I miss you more than I can say. I am so sad. But there are such wonderful people alive in the world and you keep throwing them in my path. I'm beginning to get the message.

All my love,
Martha

## 1 January 2013—12:01 A.M.

Dearest darling,

Fireworks going on outside the bedroom window. Myra saws logs on her mat near the bed. I'll turn off the light and look for you in my dreams. You are still inside every breath I take.

Went to Alice and Eddie's for supper tonight. Lovely to be with a sister and brother-in-law who have known us all our grown-up lives. It's strange to think that forty-nine years of "us" will be something new people will never know about. Something so important to me will mean nothing to them.

Going to our Eden place at Pelican Lake next summer without you will be difficult—the town is full of lonely widows. The day after you died I scribbled on a scrap of paper: "I promise to live my life with dangerous attention to my heart." Seemed mysterious at the time, but maybe it's about facing death and embracing life in equal measures, a trick, I'm discovering, that's pretty hard to do. Anyway, it's certain that I can't embrace five or six months of isolation in our summer place. I'll have to find ways of being there where I have new beginnings, look at things with fresh eyes.

Quite frequently in your last months you said, "Same old, same old." Reading was no longer available to you. Language became a trap. You couldn't follow movies. TV was the same old and watching the news the same thing. I know that you travelled in your mind and I could almost always reach in and find what you needed so we could bring it out and look at it. But I find that I can't engage in the news, now, either—or books or music. The world has gone on without you. How dare it!

I love you. Love you. Love you. That was never the same old for us. I still feel the peace of being with you. It was heart deep.

See you in my dreams, darling.


## 1 January 2013 — 9:45 P.M.

Dearest Brian,

I'm not one for New Year's resolutions, and you're not, either. Seems you've given me one, anyway. That 2013 (thirteen was once my lucky number) should be a year of taking care of myself and doing for me whatever it takes to keep me healthy and at the very least make a stab at mending my broken spirit and heart.

I spent part of the day looking at photos that you had downloaded onto the computer—ones that I thought were lost. There are even short movie clips, you behind the camera, where I can hear you laughing. In one you are following behind me as I sashay, unaware, down Dry Weather Road near our Eden place. I hear the crunch of gravel under our feet, see your shadow shift along beside me, hear you breathing, hear a quick gasping chuckle from you as I notice I'm being observed.

I made supper for Kirsten and Mike and me tonight. They've moved in to watch over me.

At one point or another, it all blurs. Kirsten said, "I know you, Mom. You won't want to live. We're here to make sure you do."

Her meaning's clear to me: "We know you wouldn't consciously try to harm yourself, but you don't seem to care if something happens, either … a tad distracted when you're out driving or when you walk in front of traffic, and so on and so forth."

She's right, I don't care. But they care. Which means I have to make an effort, if only for them.

Anyway, here we are, all of us, regrouping and doing the best we can.

All my love,
Martha


### 3 January 2013 — 7:37 A.M.

Darling Brian,

At the hospital, that first time, you confided in your old friend, Nancy, that you were afraid I'd stop writing and singing altogether. "Brian," she said, trying to reassure you, "that's the last thing Martha cares about right now."

True. But of course we all knew that you were thinking about so many things that had marked our lives, not the least of which was the fact that some of your most cherished work, especially in the last decade of your life, was as my mentor and manager.

And so, your desire that I keep on with the jazz singing and scout out a few gigs, has, I guess been working away on me.

I woke up this morning, after a (mainly) sleepless night, with the song "All the Way" in my head. The lyrics of that old chestnut spoke to me more deeply than they ever have. Who is the lyricist?

I padded down the hall and googled the song and came up with Sammy Cahn. The song is a deep anthem to a life-long love. But Cahn has also written an incredible number of other gorgeous pieces: "I Fall in Love too Easily," "Come Fly with Me," "Day by Day," "Time after Time," "The Things We Did Last Summer," "Guess I'll Hang My Tears out to Dry," "Only Trust Your Heart," "I Should Care," "Teach Me Tonight," "The Second Time Around"— my God, what a genius! A singer could do a whole album of just his songs. Or at the very least a concert. So, okay, you've got me thinking.

All my love,
Martha

### 9:28 P.M.

P.S. I just finished reading all the love letters you wrote to me in the summer of '64 when you went west for a vacation with your mother and sister Maureen and little brother Allan. Every letter started with, "Darling Martha." We met in 1963 and married in 1967, so you see we've been "Darling" to each other for a very long time. I need to remind myself that forty-nine years of life doesn't get erased in a month—or ever.

### 4 January 2013—9:00 A.M.

My darling Brian,

I got up this morning after having had the most peaceful night since your spirit left your body. I didn't so much dream of you, it went deeper than that. It felt as if I was inside your dream and therefore inside you. At one point I was dressed in a Nehru jacket and flowing pants. I remembered this morning that I owned such a jacket when we were first married and you loved it on me—such soft touchable material in psychedelic colours. You took several pictures of me in it as I walked along a stretch of beach at Clear Lake, where we honeymooned.

Reading your letters last night brought me such solace, honey.

I'll pull them out tonight when I'm in bed and read them again. In one you talked about the song "Some Enchanted Evening" and how "the words just got to me." Even back then you heard lyrics as deeply as you heard music. In another letter you mentioned that everywhere you went there were couples and that made you even more lonely for me. We'd been dating about ten months.

Loving you with all my heart,
Martha


P.S. 9:27 P.M.
Darling, alone with you in our bed is the only time I feel normal. I go through the motions. Went to see My Maureen today (as opposed to your sister, whom we've always called Our Maureen). Anyway, what a great friend of thirty years is the playwright and my soul sister Maureen Hunter. We sat in her upstairs sunroom and drank tea and talked and I cried. She told me, with all of her great gentle kindness, "You are so wise, Martha. You've given me great advice over the years and been such a comfort to me. It's simply payback time."

She and I are taking a yoga class together at the end of the month. It's a stab at putting one foot forward. I'm tired tonight. Grief is physically tiring. Rock me to sleep, my spirit love.

xox Martha


## 5 January 2013 — 8:52 A.M.

Darling, checking out this morning's news. Writing bug strikes the talented Tony Bennett. Headline reads, "Bennett writes as smooth as he croons." The reviewer of *Life Is a Gift: The Zen of Bennett* goes on to share what Bennett writes about love—that he thinks it is the most important word, of any language, and that Bennett pours his heart into work, and also friendship and family.

Thoughts to live by, honey. Unlike us he's been married three times. But, truly, maybe third time was a charm and all the more power to him. You gotta love love.

xox Martha

## 6 January 2013

Brian honey,

Woke up this morning, exhausted, and stood in front of the mirror in the bathroom you built twelve years ago with such artful attention to every detail of comfort and beauty. I could hear you say to me, just the way you would do, "You are a beautiful woman and you have your health, your life—you almost died in 2007, for heaven's sake. What a Christmas that was. But you were back to writing in January, and singing in March, and getting breast can- cer again in June and radiation and so on and you didn't once give up or say 'Why me,' and here you are. You survived, what a sur- prise, and I didn't. What are you going to do with the rest of your life? Just look at the way you connect with people and that's such a gift—don't waste it."

And yet Old Man Sorrow steals away my joy, honey, and, at times, drains my gratitude. I've been thinking a lot about mem- ory. We had memories that played in the background as we went along being together, doing beautifully normal everyday things. Walking, talking—good talks—cooking and generally minding the day. But now we've stopped our daily living. There are no more memories to be made together except through these heart-full letters to you. I'll continue to write them, con- tinue to connect with your spirit in this loving and healing way because what else can I do? I hear you say, "So keep writing, then." Oh, yes, you bet I'll write. I'll fill these pages with the life of you and me. We're still hip-to-hip.

All my love,
Martha

## 7 January 2013

Darling,

Around the time you died, Kirsten's many friends rallied around. Well, they're more than just her friends—in a way they are part of our extended family. To many we've been almost like second parents. They love the openness we've always shown them.

Jay, a member of their long ago disbanded "Not Gettin' Any" comedy troupe, and now a Lutheran pastor, conducted at our urging an off-the-wall memorial service. It was good for everybody. It's good to laugh.

Beth, now a teacher at The Pas, who calls us Maw and Paw (as many of them do), gave a eulogy about potato chips, olestra and the dissertation at our dinner table, one time, that included the phrase "anal leakage." She brought the house down. Jay, straight-faced, informed the congregation that he'd never before used those exact words in a service. Owen, standing up to give another eulogy, fumbling with some papers, goofing off as he fought to stay composed, declared, "Brian—was a cross-dresser. No … sorry … that was on the back of my Visa bill. Right—here we are." Dave, resplendent in a black suit, guitar slung across his ample chest, sang Leonard Cohen's "Hallelujah" and it was another show-stopper. Shandra, a photographer, put together a masterful slide show with music, including Monty Python's "Always Look on the Bright Side of Life" and called it, "The Life of Brian—Shit Happens!" echoing your favourite expression of the past year, "Shit happens—and there you have it."

Days after the funeral everyone was still checking in, coming over, and generally adding their good energy to our days and nights.

"Brian, in spirit, has a request," I said to Aaron, working actor and ex–car salesman, and another of Kirsten's dear friends, who bonded with you in the old days over cars and back issues of *Car and Driver*.

He eased himself into a chair beside me and said, "Shoot."

After that we talked and then he went home and researched a lot of cars and we talked some more.

This afternoon we headed off to look at the car I'd been pretty much set on getting in the first place—a hatchback that would be useful for getting things back and forth to the lake: a 2012 Toyota Matrix.

Dealing, of course is a blast, it's all a big play-acting poker game. Over the years I've come to love it. One of the things you told me, Brian, was, "Never show them your hand. And, no matter what, be absolutely prepared to walk away."

Aaron and I had already talked about that, too. It was an attitude he, himself, had adopted many times as he tried to help friends purchase their own cars. "But I've watched so many of them cave in at the last minute just because they want the car so bad."

I got this mental image of him banging his head on a desk, somewhere, his efforts to get somebody a deal completely gone up in smoke.

So, just before we walked into the dealership, I said, playfully, "Today you'll be my beloved nephew. Let's get this show on the road."

"Right," he said with a chuckle. "And, by the way, that 2012 parked over there—I'll bet it's the only one on the lot."

"It's white," I said.

I'd been thinking, somehow, orange.

"It's sharp," he countered. "And would you be willing to pay a couple of thousand more for a different colour?"

"God, no," I said.

Hand on my back, holding open the door, he ushered me inside.

Anyway, the car, once I got behind the wheel, was amazing. The steering wheel is delicious—like a race car. Aaron and I swooned over how smoothly it drives and how it hugs the road. We could feel you with us, smiling away. However, we didn't crack a smile when we dropped it off and went back inside.

Over the course of our negotiations, I kept up my end of the bargain, refusing to be charmed, unimpressed—indeed, ever so slightly bored—deferring at all times to my "beloved nephew," who played his hand very, very well.

Our salesman wheedled and carried on for quite a while before he finally went off in a sweat to see his manager.

Leaning back in his chair, Aaron said, "This car is an embarrassment to them. The only 2012 left on the lot and they've got to get rid of it. It's January and things are real slow around here. He's already knocked off seven thousand—that's about as far as he's going to go. So, you want this?"

"Absolutely."

"A cargo net would be nice. We're going to ask them to eat the tax and pony up the cargo net."

"Right on."

We walked away with a sealed deal.

As we were leaving, Aaron, thrilled by the whole experience, said to me, "You just kept puttin' it up on the shelf there."

"You mean I'm good at this?"

"Oh, yeah," he said with an ear-to-ear grin. "It was sweet. I had the most fun I've had in a long time."

"Me, too," I said gleefully.

We left the car behind until Monday, when he'll come with me to pick it up and make sure all is in order. I took him out to The Keg for a steak, which he didn't expect, but that's the way you would have done it, and he was so pleased and we were both hungry. We were together from 2:00 until 8:00 and I found a piece of you in him, and he found a sense of home in us again.

"You and Brian were the cool parents," he said. "You were the parents we all wanted." He also said that your memorial service had been magical. "I was so happy to be there. He was a true gentleman—that's a rarity in this world. He was somebody to emulate and look up to."

A wonderful day, all in all, honey.

All my love,
Martha

## 8 January 2013

Darling Brian,

Another day without you. The world goes on. I go on. I know I'm lucky, have been lucky, but at the end of the day I'm still without you. That's never going to change. I love you inside memory, inside my body, as outside I am strangely alone. Every conversation I have now is edged with my singularity and even should I be lucky enough to find somebody, somewhere, some day, you will still be the echo I long for.

Loving you with every beat of my heart,
Martha

## 9 January 2013

Darling,

As I look over my journal entries from last year the thing that comes up over and over is gratitude. Yet, while the miracle of having made it through an entire year with you, after you were diagnosed, is absolutely something to be grateful for, I am not grateful that you were taken from me. We should have gone gently into our old age together. Instead, I'll have this new car and you won't be beside me and so I go on into a very uncertain Brian-less future. Travel with me, honey. Shadow my days in music and writing and give me your arms in my dreams.

All my love,
Martha


## 11 January 2013 – 11:50 P.M.

Darling Brian,

Tonight, it's snowing—a clean quiet blanket covers the city. Beneath our bedroom window, the Matrix (I've christened him Rabbit) sits under a thick layer of it. I've found you in the newness of that car. Your pleasure in experiencing any lovely new vehicle was there this afternoon as Kirsten and I drove in a blizzard towards Beaudry Park. "You're going to have a great time, Mom," she said. "You're going to have years of pleasure in this car." She loves the solace of driving. I think I may join her in that. Our daughter carries some of your energy, some of mine. What a gift she is and what a comfort. Beautiful, what we created, you and me.

All my love,
Martha


## 12 January 2013

Brian honey,

Writing to you—this is how I make it through. It's one of the sanest things I've done and I'm doing for myself since you died. It keeps me steady (your hand on my back) and keeps me travelling through grief, which in actual fact is not a state—it's a continent. I look back at a kind of trajectory of (very) surprising rises in mood and then real low down dips, but the words do tell me that progress is being made. I'm lucky to be an artist, to be able to take shelter in this, my muscular art form, to make life on the page as a way through soul-scraping pain. Your gifts to me just keep coming. For all the things you are and have been to me, thank you.

All my love,
Martha

14 January 2013

Sweetheart,

A good day of writing. Mid-afternoon, in the way that you and I always would do, I loaded the dog in the (new) car and went to the dog park—haven't been there for a while. Our day, yours and mine, certainly in recent years, always centred on the walk. Me, writing in the morning, the walk, and then home, where you gathered things together to make supper. We were so self-sufficient in the way that that was all we needed, just to be together doing the extraordinarily ordinary things. All we needed, really, was the equation of us. But now the number is one. What do you do with one? It's the same old grief, my life stretching ahead without you. There is no end to sorrow. Certainly no "closure"—God, how we've both hated that stupid word and the half-baked notions it engenders in perfectly nice people.

So I listen to recordings of me singing—not to hear my own voice, but to swim in the knowledge that you were there as all that lovely music was being made, you were so much part of it.

And I search for scraps of paper with your handwriting—old grocery lists, measurements of walls and floors in this unfinished house, a small stick-it note where you wrote "Ciao!" and stuck it to your computer and now it's on my iBook where I can see it every morning as I start writing.

I have a green notebook where I've written about all the thinking and planning for this new novel. It's peppered with things you said, advice you gave, and now I wish it was filled with your thoughts—not to mention your handwriting.

I seek you everywhere. Find solace in fleeting things. This morning as I was waking, somewhere between the cracks of slumber and dream, we had a conversation. I don't remember what it was about—just that we had one. I'm calmer than I was, even as I live this life without you yet very much still with you. I'm finding ways to heal, little patches, with patches on the patches. I love you, you walk with me no matter where I go. You shadow me, like dusk on a summer day, warmly.

All my love,
Martha


## 17 January 2013 —7:28 P.M.

Darling Brian,

Last year on this date I wrote in my journal: "Brian said to me today, 'We've had a pretty good run at it and we're not done, yet.'"

Called your sister, Our Maureen. She remembered that January 17, 1957 was the day your dad died. It's an anniversary that she's always remembered.

Right from the time I met you, you had a seemingly stoic view of death. I remember the sadness I felt for you, as the young twenty-year-old man I'd just met, when you told me about your father dying when you were thirteen and then a year or so later your best friend Derry and his father (your surrogate father) were killed in a plane crash. Such unimaginable early sorrow, such trauma. I had a hard time wrapping my head around how that all must have looked for you.

After you were diagnosed you were still (except for the time when steroids controlled you) pretty stoic. You believed you weren't going to die anytime soon. ("We're not done yet.") Besides, your diagnosis didn't mean we threw up our hands and gave up on living. We soldiered on, living each moment as hopefully as we could. That isn't unrealistic, it's heroic. However, in June, we were lying in bed together and I said, "I promise you that you're the only one—the only one for me. I'll wait for you until we're both on the other side and I'll come and find you."

You pulled away on the pillow, held me in a surprised and tearful gaze and said, "But I'll be gone!"

Not more than a day after you were diagnosed you said to Mike, "A year or two, she'll meet somebody—some nice guy." When Mike reported this back to me I almost dropped and then I fell apart.

I realize, now, you were just taking care of me. Three big wishes: writing, singing and, dear God, a boyfriend.

Case in point, we've lived in the same townhouse complex since 1979, a lot of living has strolled beneath our kitchen window—among them new widows and widowers—and it wasn't unusual for you to turn from buttering your morning toast to say something like, "Looks like _____ had a sleepover last night. It's about time. Good for her."

The summer before you got sick, on a hot July evening that clings to my memory, we got in the air-conditioned car, drove to one of our favourite walking places, then just crawled along, the gravel pinging under the tires. We had a conversation as we rolled past cottonwood trees, their limbs raised in Hallelujah against the sky.

I remember saying, "I'm grateful to be inside this moment with you. I want to hold onto it. Someday there'll just be one of us—God forbid it's sooner rather than later."

"We could always go out together," you said, playfully squeezing my knee. "Right here. Blaze of glory."

"I'm serious, honey."

"Well," you said, glancing up into the trees, "it's not going to happen for a long time."

"But if it did—what I need to say is I'd want the one of us who was left behind to be happy."

I said this because I felt almost certain it would be you, alone, and not me.

"So I guess you're telling me that the odds are we won't go out together," you said with a chuckle. "Too bad. I always thought it'd be kind of neat."

"I know," I smiled, "you're so bizarre."

"And so, failing that, whoever is left behind will need to find some kind of life, Martha—we've seen it over and over again with people, right?"

You continue to take care of me with, among other things, these crowded memories. The thing is, honey, I can't imagine anyone but you. To be fair, I'm having a hard time imagining my life, period, without you.

It's one day at a time, sometimes one hour at a time. Let me just say this: I'm wrapped forever in your heart; you are my home.

All my love,
Martha


19 January 2013—8:10 A.M.

Darling Brian,

Sitting at the table this morning, having breakfast in winter's dark by candlelight. I remember all the times we sat side by side at this table, European street style, just as we did in Paris in September 2004. We sat side by side there and here, as well as at our Eden place overlooking the weather and the seasons, the sky and long expanse of lake.

"Nothing left on the bucket list," I wrote in the cottage journal the summer before you were diagnosed, "except, of course, several more summers out here with my man."

How often did I turn to you, especially in those dozen years you had after you retired, and say, "I'm grateful for this, for us, for this moment in time here with you, for this lovely life we are living." We were blessed to possess the knowledge (especially after I "died" and came back to you in 2007) that our time together was not to be taken lightly.

Yesterday, Michelle Grégoire, the first jazz pianist who truly gave a home to my jazz voice, called from Calgary—such a lovely surprise—and she reminded me about a moment between you and me the last time she came for supper, just before she moved from Winnipeg. It was spring 2011—seven months before you were diagnosed. She was standing in the kitchen with us. "You were such an inspiration to me as a couple," she said. "You looked at each other, Martha, as you said, 'You have to be grateful, to be aware that life could throw you a curve and it all could end.'" She went on, "The way Brian looked at you when you said that—as if he was thinking that he almost didn't have you, you were so sick, and it could happen again. I don't think any of us thought that it would be him that would go first."

xox M.

## 20 January 2013

Brian honey,

Remember how you and I used to joke, on days when neither one of us was functioning, "Together, we have a complete brain." And then, God help us, after you were diagnosed I had to think and do for us both. Sometimes that was overwhelming. I remember one day at the cottage when we had to be somewhere and I was rushing you. I stopped in the middle of it all and turned to you, weeping, and said, "Oh, God, I'm so sorry," and you put both hands on my shoulders and held me that way and looked at me and said, "Martha, it's okay. You have a lot on your plate."

But I also remember—as fondly as if it were happening now—the daily discussion of your eye drops. You'd come out of the bedroom and say, "Now I have to do something."

41

"Right, darling, your eye drops."

"Ah, right—where are they?"

"The bedroom."

You'd disappear into the bedroom and (usually) locate them. I found that increasingly marvellous, because your location of things as the disease progressed was a bit dodgy.

So then you'd reappear, eye drops in hand.

"That was my left eye."

"No, darling, your right."

"Ah, yes."

Into the bathroom, but soon, head appearing around the corner, "My—left eye."

"No, darling, your right."

"Did I take my pills?"

"Yep, I have your back, big time."

"I'm so forgetful."

"I don't care, darling. Ask me a hundred times a day about anything. I'll answer you every single time, delighted to do it— right eye."

There was something so endearing in the way you operated. After the eye drops there was breakfast, everything lined up exactly. Never mess with a brain tumour patient's mind, as it is messed up enough already.

"And the toaster is …?"

"Right behind you, darling."

"Right!"

These days I try to find comfort and sanity in asking myself, "What would Brian do in this situation?" It helps me go on in this Brian-less life. Helps me think for two and live for two and just be for two, even as I walk this slender singular path. Oh yes, your hand still on my back, steadying me.

All my love,
Martha

## 22 January 2013

Darling,

Yesterday was not a good day. Because of it I didn't pick up a pen—not to write a letter to you or to work on the novel. It's a bad idea not to write, because then I spiral down and it's hard to move.

I forced myself to vacuum today and then to make supper as I do a couple of times a week for Kirsten and Mike and me—neither of which anybody expects—but I find that it fills the time and helps to keep me upright.

I'm so grateful to have them here. They are playful and wise and don't care if I'm in Crazy Town, or pretty good, or just boarding the Crazy Train for Crazy Town, where, they explain, "You have your own dining car and they serve you margaritas. It's lovely."

I told them that I now have a mansion in Crazy Town.

"With gingerbread siding," Kirsten offered, "and spinning candy canes at the front door. By the way, this quiche is absolutely delicious."

I went to bed early. A little later, after Mike had headed off too (he'd be getting up at 5:00 a.m to do an overnighter in Brandon), the phone rang. I picked up in your office and Kirsten picked up in the basement, where she was doing laundry.

It was Mike, calling us from their bedroom. He was delighted that Kirsten and I had both picked up.

"Hello," we all said. "Hello? Hello, hello! Who's there? Hello, it's me. Is that you?" And then a couple of silly insults ending with a *Waltons*-esque, "Good night, John Boy!" We'd just finished watching *The Return of the Pink Panther*—the good one with the dentist scene and the laughing gas. I remember how hard you laughed when we saw it in 1976 when it first came out.

In bed, now, I've pulled a couple of your letters out of the orange cardboard scarf box—they are all still tied together with black ribbon, same ribbon I used in the summer of 1964 when you sent them. In one you said, "I miss you so much, sweetheart," and then signed as you always did, "All my love, Brian," and a p.s. with "sweet dreams."

xox Martha

Early A.M.—I'm not sure that my dreams were sweet. I wish I could remember them. One day I will. One day I'll actually see you in one of them. Meanwhile, last night I did sleep better and that was a godsend.

I love you, my darling, with every cell of my being. It's not much fun without you, but I'm trying to have it anyway. You want me to. And, God knows, Kirsten and Mike do too.

All my love,
Martha

## 23 January 2013

Darling,

Today I had a rehearsal with Jeff Presslaff. Sat in his presence for the first ten minutes and wept. Said I was sorry and he said, "Why are you sorry?"

Told him I didn't know if I should be applying to the Jazz Festival this year and, anyway, maybe I was wasting his time—who would want to come out and hear me, anyway?

He levelled me with a look and said, "Two years ago you packed the place. And you work with good people. Everybody does Johnny Mercer, nobody does Sammy Cahn—so I think it's a great idea and you should apply."

He proceeded to make a list of eighteen great Sammy Cahn songs and to put them all in my key. As I was leaving I told him I felt much better than when I arrived and thanked him.

"You're welcome," he said. "Listen, I know your writing gives you shelter but it isn't good to hide away. You need to be with people. Music can help with that."

I try to be wise and patient, to believe that things will get better, and today they did.

All my love,
M.

## 24 January 2012—9:19 P.M.

Brian, you were my champion, my protector, and my biggest fan—in other words, irreplaceable. The world is a helluva lonely place without you. Dear God—how do I sing those love songs without you here to sing them to? Do I sing about of how you keep my love young and new in "Time After Time"? How about "The Things We Did Last Summer," when there are no more summers? Or, all those good and lean years and all those in-between years in "All the Way"? Do I get up on that stage and your face is not out there cheering me on, and sing from my broken heart about "Come Fly with Me" and some boozy bar in Bombay? Maybe I'll just go walk off a fucking pier. Except all the lakes are frozen. Endlessly sad. I'd say I'm just feeling sorry for myself, but that wouldn't be much of a compliment to Old Man Sorrow, who has done such a fine job down here on earth. God, honey. Well, I love you, wherever the hell you are. And I never forget to write.

All my love, and I mean it,
Martha

## Sunday, 3 February, 2013 10:14 P.M.

Brian, such a bad day of soul-sucking sorrow. Pushed through it anyway, from a writing session, to a walk with your brother and the dogs in wintry Assiniboine Forest, to cooking Sunday supper—Italian meat loaf, red sauce, polenta, salad, chocolate butterscotch pie, red wine—and having family time with Kirsten and Mike.

Kirsten is taking some time away from her job and is on her way tomorrow, driving to California with Shandra. Mike's happy that she's getting this well-deserved holiday and so am I. However at the end of the day, even in her excitement at taking one of her beloved and healing road trips, the ever-present undercurrent of grief pulled us both under.

We cuddled up in the kitchen as she said, "I still can't believe he's gone. He was so healthy. It was such a shock. It just broadsided us."

But then, later, I overheard her on the phone with Shandra as she resurfaced, again, with a goofy memory of you: "I'm surprised any of my friends ever came back to the house after they met the family," she said, playfully. "I'm opening the door. Dad's up in the living room next to the speakers, listening to Tibetan music—The Gyuto Monk Chants—and he's got his eyes closed and he's nodding his head and the monks are going, "Nyuh la wahhh wahhh loooooooooooooow."

She came away from the phone and told me, "We're taking the Gyuto Monk's CD to Death Valley and we're going to crank it just for Dad."

Such is the continent of grief, and the courage and curiosity and resilience of its travellers as they strap on those heavy backpacks and go down its bumpy roads.

Your ever-loving wife,
Martha


4 February 2013 – 10:17 P.M.

My darling Brian,

Listened at close range to Patricia Barber's new CD *Smash* while I was having supper tonight. Probably not the brightest thing I could have done—braised salmon and tears are an unsavoury mix. But then I would have missed "Spring Song." In your own words, "No one writes lyrics like her."

Indeed:

his absence
fills the pail
like water
to the brim
April comes
and winter
gardens grow
without him

Gone. Gone. Gone. Your absence fills this house, spills into the void, slips through me. Just when I think I'm done, for an hour or two, with sorrow, it comes and finds me. So this is grief. No cheerful smiles, no perky keeping on with admirable positivism. Just me and grief and the oh so familiar taste of tears.

And, oh, how I love you, my love—
Martha

## 5 February 2013 —Tuesday, 9:55 P.M.

Brian, my darling. A day that started tearfully, but by evening, after supper with Mike and Aaron and then sitting around talking about cars (I love talking about cars) I started to feel more normal, less lost without you. The writing went well, too. More and more I find you inside it. However, I guess the hardest thing now is the gradual dawning of the idea that you are never coming back—not physically. You aren't, like our darling daughter, taking a road trip. You haven't gone away on your own vacation—you are completely, irrevocably, gone from our lives, and no matter how many letters I write to you, they will never be returned.

I write them anyway.

At one point during the year you were sick, you did say, with a kind of sobbing glee, "When this is all over, you'll really have something to write about."

"God, darling, don't say that."

Ah, but Brian, you were right.

Always in my heart,
Martha


6 February 2013 – 3:15 P.M.

Darling Brian,

Your diagnosis just came out of nowhere: inoperable glioblastoma. This secret enemy that was growing in your brain gave us very little indication. I noticed a slight tremor in your hands which you dismissed if ever I brought it up, and there was a forgetfulness that I chalked up to age—hell, we were both forgetful. Sometimes you couldn't locate things and I'd find them for you. When I look back at photos taken of you at the lake in the summer of 2010, you didn't quite look yourself, but then you were dealing with arthritis.

What was so unbelievable to all of us, this horrible diagnosis, and what we all knew would happen—it was just a matter of when—was that even after we knew you were sick you almost always looked well. You'd say, "I feel well. I sleep more but I've always been a good sleeper."

And as the tumour seemed to stabilize and go dormant like a sleeping dragon, we tried to go on with our lives.

There was no pain, not physical at least, and you looked forward to each day—especially at the lake—such a blessing—May 1st to October 25th, which was almost six months. During that time, when you could no longer read, you'd "look" at the paper, and when we went for walks you'd look at the landscape, the weather, and me as if we were the greatest gifts of your life.

When you were in hospital for the last time—when we'd had to haul you out of here by ambulance because you discovered, one morning, that you could no longer walk—you said to me in a sunny room at the Acute Care Ward, "This all happened so fast."

"Yes, it did," I said. "Unbelievable."

And yet the morning they took you out I knew it was over.

Your wedding ring shines up at me from the middle finger of my right hand. The ring with "Brian loves Martha, August 26, 1967" inscribed inside. We could never remember our anniversary—was it the 26th or the 27th? But I'll always remember you died on the 27th of November at 9:27 A.M. I wear both rings now as a tribute to our marriage and against the loneliness of my Brian-less life.

Writing to you prolongs this life we had together. A kind of tragic addendum.

And yet my mood swings up. I wrote well today—you and me inside the novel that now seems to be ours.

My Maureen had a dream about you last night. In it we were all together at her house. You looked well and happy, she said, and you were giving her the most intricate suggestions for her own writing. She kept scribbling them down, all over the food, all over everything, so she wouldn't forget your advice.

Our nephew, Brian, had a similar dream in Montreal around Christmas. Somewhere between his teaching duties with young playwrights at the National Theatre School and everything else he does, he was catching some sleep and had a dream where you came to him, rappelling out of the sky, all beautiful arms and legs, and gave him the entire plot for the mid-section of a storyline that he's working on for a Cirque du Soleil show. He woke up in the morning, wrote it out, said, "By God, he's right!" and sent it off to the storyboard people, who wrote back to say, "This is fantastic!"

I told Maureen that even though you were a frustrated artist, you were an artist nonetheless, and now that you are free-floating you can pop in and be everybody's muse. Maureen said, "I think

49

we should fire our other muse—the one we dreamed up who's always swilling Scotch in Florida and won't speak to us and doesn't want to get out of bed before noon—and hire Brian."

I must admit, when I got off the phone with her, I had shivers and chills, as if there was a direct message from you saying, "Yes! That's exactly what I want!"

You amaze me.

All my love,
Martha


7 February 2013 — 9:26 A.M.

On a very odd note, darling,

I had a dream last night that was not about you, it was about Al Pacino. Now that I think about this, you'll get a kick out of it. So there I am, somewhere with Al Pacino. He's looking quite dapper and seventy-something, or whatever the heck he is, and wearing normal clothes—sweater, chinos, loafers—and I'm wearing something equally normal looking. Anyway, we strike up a conversation and go for coffee and then just walk along the street, talking, and I'm thinking what a lovely man he is, just a very nice person. Anyway, he stops in the middle of the sidewalk, turns and kisses me. It's a lovely kiss. I'm quite pleased by it. But I feel it's only fair to tell him, "You'd be number two."

"Oh, that's okay," he says, and pats my back.

How goofy. And then I woke up. So now your rival is Al Pacino. Or not.

The Taoists say it takes a lifetime to get to know somebody and I'm still getting to know you.

On another note, Mike's been puttering around cleaning up the garage. What a wonderful thing to do. Last night he came into the basement where I was watching TV and announced, "Brian is brilliant."

"I know he is," I said.

"I just found a whole bag of parquet flooring he'd been saving. I am going to painstakingly glue it back into that circle on your bedroom floor where the Japanese tub will now not be going."

In this, our half-finished house, there are many handsome corners that you designed and built. Which means, among many other things, a fireplace set inside a wall with floor-to-ceiling step-ups like a Navajo blanket zigzag. Then there is my loft-like office with its yellow bookshelves and sunny walls and the wondrous sky with clouds that you painted on the ceiling. Yes, and the upstairs bathroom looks like something from *Architectural Digest*. But then, of course, there are the other corners: the torn-up downstairs bathroom, the kitchen with the stripped wallpaper and terrible floor and holes in one wall. The upstairs master bedroom, which you were readying for the Japanese tub—part of the project that is too daunting for the rest of us to complete. The room was double drywalled for soundproofing (but it never did get painted).

Ah well, the soundproofing scarcely matters now, as there is nothing very interesting going on in our bed. I write my head off and try to say afloat in the grief boat. It's not the same as *The Love Boat*, honey, but maybe it's a close cousin, as you are always in my heart and you swim through me.

All my love,
Martha

## 9 February — 10:28 P.M.

Brian, how strange life is. Just the very thing of you not being here, of life continuing without you. I try to wrap my head around that lonely concept every single day. I live my life—without you. Sleep without you, see the world through eyes that gathered you in and existed side by side with you.

When our beloved Airedale, Drummer, died, you told me,

"The house is so quiet." She filled a room, of course, with all her headlong joy. Her loss affected you deeply. Imagine, now, how I'm feeling. Oh honey, it brings me to my knees. How would you have handled this if it had been me who was gone and you left behind? I try to picture it, and I see you lonely, possibly shut in on yourself, but I also think that like me you'd eventually want to reach out and connect with people. And not be a pain in the neck.

I sometimes find myself angry at the complacency I see around me. Couples just going on about their lives while life itself is a ticking time bomb. They think they're safe as they go out for dinner, to a movie, comfortable in their skin and (if they are a loving couple) comfortable with each other. Life. Just. Goes. On. I am a woman suddenly alone. I don't know how to behave, how to walk with this awkward amputation oozing from my side where you used to be joined to me. Nobody wants to look at that for long. Widowhood is a Medusa with snakes for hair. So then I cheer up, put on a smile, make myself attractive, disappear inside the way grief softens me and makes me beautiful (all that vulnerability, apparently) to some and a goddamn pain in the ass to others. Too bad this widowhood thing didn't happen to me later. At sixty-eight I am unbelievably and inconveniently unmoored.

Tonight I'm angry—your normally hopeful wife. This will pass. I'll go along and cry and smile and laugh and pray to the stars and occasionally look forward to what might yet be, when what was, was so comfortable and beautiful and ordinary—like you in the dark, breathing beside me.

All my love, my darling husband,
Your heartbroken wife, Martha

"WE CAN ONLY BE SAID TO BE ALIVE IN THOSE MOMENTS WHEN OUR HEARTS ARE CONSCIOUS OF OUR TREASURES."
—THORNTON WILDER

## Monday, 11 February 2013 — 6:50 P.M.

Brian darling,

This letter to you is entitled "Counting My Blessings Without My Darling Husband of 45 Years."

I am grateful for a healthy body that keeps me going

— without you

I am grateful for good food and a beautiful roof over my head, both enjoyed

— without you

I am grateful for our daughter who loves me enough to move in with me and keep a watchful eye over me, while we are both sorrowing

— without you

I am grateful for our (sometimes) baffled son-in-law who loves Kirsten enough to move in with her mother and keep a watchful eye over us both (while we both sorrow in different ways) and keeps his head and his playfulness and his sense of humour while the three of us go on

— without you

I am grateful for friends and other family who call and come around, their eyes brimming with sadness and (sometimes) admiration, while life goes on

— without you

I am grateful for the shelter of my art in which I (often) find you and which is all the more tender and raw

— without you

I am grateful for snow and the seasons, the moon, the sun, the stars and the spring which will (inevitably) come

— without you

I am grateful for all the years we had together, for the sweetness of your spirit, for the bigness of your arm-spreading love, for all the things that we were to each other, for the things we said, and the things we didn't, for respect and cherishing and moments of quiet wonderment and comfort, all sadly behind me

—without you

## 12 February 2013—8:49 P.M.

Darling Brian,

A day of ordinary emotion, few tears. Had a massage. Went to Alice's book club, home to have supper, get Myra for a walk around the block and then, feeling blessedly sleepy, an hour in front of the TV as Barack Obama gave his State of the Union Address. How many times have you and I listened intently to him, but tonight his familiar voice was like a lullaby and I have no idea what he said.

Earlier in the evening Dog Park Dennis called, trying to roust me out for walks "with the gang." He says he's going to keep bugging me. When he asked how I was doing, I was honest.

"Well that's love, Love—that's what it is," he said in his Liverpool accent. "I used to enjoy watching you and Brian. You were so in sync—you two would often notice and comment on the same things at the same time. It was a pleasure to be around. You were a great couple. Give it time, Martha—come out with me and the guys. It's good for the dogs and all of us."

I said I'd think about it. I'm going to sleep, now. Kind of beat, I must say.

Wrapped inside the warmth of your big love,
Martha

## 14 February 2013—9:05 P.M.

Darling Brian,

Last year, you and I took a little Valentine's Day road trip out to Eden. I took the trip again this year with one particularly difficult first. Stood on a wintery hill with our friend Marilyn, up to our knees in snow as we looked down at the cottage roof. I thought about how our life there was once so easy—I was spoiled by your easy caress, by the softness of skin-to-skin, by the lightness of my heart, the bliss of well-being, sighing contentedly beside you, counting our blessings (always). You were a moment away from my touch, my glance, from the ordinary enjoyment of the way the light slanted across the landscape, the way the sun embraced any little thing between us, from your voice, so dear to me, now gone.

Happy Valentine's Day, my darling. The sweetness of my thoughts follows you wherever you are.

On the drive home I saw an eagle at the side of the road. I think he winked.

XOX Martha

## 15 February 2013 — 9:20 P.M.

Darling Brian,

A slightly more lighthearted day—a good yoga class, a great visit with My Maureen. A trip to Costco where I chose new frames for my glasses—pretty, and it'll be nice not to see the world through scratches.

When Mike came home, around 5:00, he found me vacuuming and singing a robust rendition of "Georgia on My Mind." He was delighted to find me so cheerful. I was delighted to find me so cheerful. Your absence continues to scrape at my soul, the rawness is part of how I operate, but at least I can flood it with music and friends and new connections. One foot forward, heart cradled in my spirit. Never far from missing you. And still so very much in love with you, my man.

Embracing your spirit with every fibre of my being,
Your Martha

## Monday, 17 February 2013

Brian, last night Kirsten returned home and regaled us with stories of the wonders of Big Sur, Pebble Beach, Mount Shasta. And Death Valley: "One of the most peaceful places I've ever been." After a road trip she always looks radiant, and to see it this time was particularly lovely.

Between her and your sister Maureen, who is here for a brief visit and sleeping in the bed beside me, I slept—not well, but deeply. How could I not with all that beautiful Brooks energy: Kirsten back in the house and your sister's soft breath rising and falling beside me.

All my love, my darling man,
Martha


## 22 February 2013—6:01 P.M.

Darling Brian,

Found much solace today in music. A little session with my old jazz buddy, Glenn Buhr. I went over to his place and he played his lovely big piano and I sang. It was a balm to my aching spirit, just slipped down my interior walls like a big wash of warm honey. The love of his life, Margaret, appeared after we were done and told me, "You look wonderful."

Not sure how that happens with all I've been going through, but at least, in my singularity, I don't look as if I've been dragged through the swampy sea of grief.

You pour through my spirit—maybe that's why—you are formless now, an orange ether that flows warmly at will—like honey, like a song, like art as it is being created.

I love you,
Martha

Saturday, 23 February 2013 — 10:52 P.M.

Darling,

Every Saturday evening, brother-in-law Eddie picks me up and drives me ten blocks over to his and Alice's place where he pours me a glass of wine—always a ceremony, always very good wine, always presented just so, always tasted, appreciated, as the flow of conversation stops so I take in the ethers and sigh and feel blessed—then we have supper and watch a movie. Tonight we watched *Ladies in Lavender*. Judi Dench masterfully plays an elderly sister who has never had a love of her own.

"Dear God," I said to my own sister, "how dismal. And here I am kvetching that I only had my man adoring me since 1963. How greedy of me to want more."

"You always want more," Alice said. "There's never enough time."

I've often said the same thing. A hundred years would have been just about perfect, Brian—but even then I probably would still have been stung by the unfairness of it all.

Today I worked on the novel for eight hours! You were with me the whole time. I was flushed and in love by the end of the day. You are a gorgeous muse. I'm not going to want to finish this book. But I hear you (giving me a nudge) saying, "You'll write another."

"But will I find you in it?"

"Of course you will. You're just getting started. We're just getting started."

Goodnight my love,
Martha

27 February 2013 — 11:20 A.M.

Darling Brian,

On the anniversary of the third month since you slipped out of your body and left us, I found solace in writing, deep tears of grief holding your orange fleece jacket (that still smells of you) against my chest as I sat in the morning sunlight on the end of our red bed, and then, searching for you, anything of you, I looked through some dusty bags and found your old pocket calculator. Tucked inside were business cards relating to the year you retired and my CD *Change of Heart* was released. There was, tucked inside as well, a yellowing, Scotch Taped newspaper clipping dated May 13, 2000. It seems you carried it, like a talisman, all these years. There were words here that formed an impression of how amidst the very best of all possible times there can be the contradictory discovery that what we've thought to be true in life is wrong—that in itself can be exciting.

These were words you lived by as you made peace with your own life, with what you had thought it would be and, later, with the uncertainty of your illness. May I say, what a hero.

As I grow up in my spirit and continue making art, you continue to send these miraculous little messages that support it all. Yet here I am, stubbornly wishing for your human form.

I love you,
Martha

## 28 February 2013—9:11 P.M.

Darling Brian,

Last day of February. I am, as is true most days, a faucet. Billie Holiday would approve. I am also a woman out and about, doing things.

Went to visit our old friends Brian and Margaret MacKinnon for lunch. Margaret said you arrived before I did and turned on the vacuum cleaner just to get her attention. Their little dog, Sunny, who doesn't like the vacuum cleaner anyway, barked at its sudden spontaneous unassisted leap to life. I think he then hid. Margaret said that if ever there was anyone who could stick around and take care of business after "death" it would be you.

"His spirit was so clear," she said, "unlike the rest of us. He's right with you—I know he is—and he wants to take care of you."

Well, you have my/our attention. You know Margaret, she shifts and shimmers with this stuff. You always got such a kick out of her.

Lovely to have you surrounding me with warmth and love the way you do. I'll sink back into your spirit and turn off the light.

All my love,
Martha


## 1 March 2013 — 4:41 P.M.

Brian, another day without you and it ain't over yet. Evidently, honey, it gets better. I mostly hear this from people who've never been there. I suspect I'm in this for the long haul. Living my life making love to a ghost. Even still—as the saying goes: When I count my blessings, I count you twice.

xox M.


## 2 March 2013

Brian, I've dipped down so low this week—the ocean is deep. Here's what I think. My grief for you is about love. It's about a normally resilient and hopeful woman who has to ride this out, like giving birth—painful waves, but ultimately transforming. I'm giving birth to a new me. I think that each time I go down to the bottom of the ocean, when I come back up I'm a little stronger and things look a little better, just a little brighter.

I've also been thinking lately about dreams and how they exist side by side with our waking life—informing our journeys, healing us just as sleep heals us. I feel off-kilter and so it's necessary to embrace the dream world and go down deep into it. Are you in that world? In that altered state of being? Now that you are a free agent—and you always did love sleep—is the world of dreams your domain, your country? You didn't just disappear. The essence of you went somewhere. You have me in a state of wonder. Can I meet you somewhere for a metaphysical coffee? Some heavenly cafe where we can sit side by side as we used to do and just be together?

I love you with all my heart,
Martha


## 3 March 2013 – 7:42 A.M.

Darling Brian,

This morning, somewhere between waking and dreaming, the veil lifted. I saw you, sitting alfresco, at the head of a very long table, gloriously smiling, having the time of your life (or death, as the case may be). The table was set in an arbour of spring trees— leafy, with that lively fiery green of spring that you always loved and commented on. The air was sweet and filled with chatter and the sound of bees. The table was set with a linen cloth. There were luscious pink blossoms floating in bowls up and down that table, and food and laughter. You were tanned and handsome and happy, surrounded by friends and family, by everyone who had come to the table (must have been forty feet long) to celebrate and honour you.

I have a small regret. That we never held that kind of meal for you when you were alive. And yet, and yet, there you were telling me that this is where you are now. And then I remember all those meals we had on the deck this summer with family and friends— the tablecloth lifting in the summer breeze, the pot of flowers that you would so carefully place in the middle and the way you would pause to lift your eyes to the blue sky that framed all of us who so dearly loved you.

Your Martha


## 5 March 2013, Tuesday —9:52 P.M.

Darling,

It doesn't seem to matter what age you are or how many years you've been together, "You become one," is the operative phrase for how painful it then becomes when a close couple is no longer "one."

I suppose the one left behind just "learns to live with it"—such an odd phrase for such a severing experience. One learns to live with a psychic amputation. The place from where the beloved has been torn grows over, a fine skin, soft and mottled with grief, looking like near-death—the otherworldly, neither-here-nor-there state of waiting. And so I look at it. I look at it all. I don't distract myself from feeling the things I must feel. I love and live, as always, with dangerous attention to my heart. And because I do I keep you close to my ear, my spirit, and, ultimately, as you so wish, to my Art.

All my love,
Martha


## 9 March 2013 —11:59 P.M.

Darling Brian,

I heard from the Winnipeg Jazz Festival today with an offer for me to appear with my quartet! Evidently you've been busy giving somebody a nudge. I'm very happy about the gig, my first in a year—so pleased to make music. There are a lot of songs to prepare and a lot of that work, the charts and arranging, and so on, will be squarely on Jeff's shoulders. But he seems to be quite prepared to do it, the man is all about the music—what a gift! He's invited me out to hear him play on Tuesday and I've asked my other jazz compadre, Denis Chan, to buddy up with me for the evening. Life is a little better, altogether a little brighter. No tears today. I think that that's a first. I'm sitting in bed, wrapped up in your orange fleece—inside it, as you are inside me.

All my love,
Martha

## 12 March 2013 — 8:31 A.M.

My darling Brian,

This letter to you will be the last in this very full journal. Looking back on these past two and a half months of outpourings, I realize it's all been about my search for you. Trying to find comfort in the nebulousness of an orange ether, a formless you. I have felt, almost always during this time, that I have taken you in. Also that you shimmer in a warm glow against my flesh. I have found you in others—a gesture, a look, an act of support reminding me of all that you were to me. I have found you in synchronous events that feel very much orchestrated. Every few days, it seems you push something onto my path as if to say, "See? I'm here making things happen. Do you believe now?"

I've tried, and for the most part was unsuccessful, to find you in my dreams. No matter how much I whined and blew my nose and drowned in my own tears, you rarely showed yourself.

Until last night.

We were at the lake in our normal (and miraculous) extraordinarily ordinary way of being—the equation of you and me, of us. It was a very early spring. The snow had all melted, but it was still chilly. As we went around, opening up the place, we looked past the windows and remarked that there were flakes of snow in the air. But the water had been turned on and we were there for an overnight—to check on the place and make sure that all was in order. We put away food and looked in all the cupboards to see what we might need at The Grocery Box in Ninette.

As we chatted and moved around together with such comfort and connection, we discussed the fact that while everything would be normal with just us here at the cabin, it would be awkward when we went to town. Nobody would be able to see you. And that would be hard to explain. It was then I realized that the gift of seeing you was mine alone. At that point we made our grocery list and then got in the car and drove slowly to Ninette, enjoying the view of the lake and the hills on the other side.

We parked in front of the store, got out, went inside, and you were right behind me. I realized I'd have to stop talking to you, so I did. But you, of course, kept right on, commenting on things in your usual fashion, making trouble, deftly pinching my ass in the produce aisle. I was alarmed, but it was also so very you and so it was funny. Then you decided to talk to the proprietor, Marv. When he didn't hear you, you reached out and touched his face. Thing is, he felt it! He lurched back as if he'd been jolted. We beat it out of there pretty fast, and as for Marv, yes, of course he'd feel it: he's been touched by the same sorrow as me—his first wife died of brain cancer.

I don't remember what you and I did after that, honey, but probably we went back to the cottage where I'll find you this spring, summer and fall. As the song title says, "I'll Be Seeing You."

I woke from my dream refreshed and comforted and so thoroughly with you. My dreamscape is ready for summer memories. To wake in the morning to the sound of that woodland thrush, the veery and the Eastern towhees, the sun rising over the deck, having spent at least part of the night with you in the blessed scented wind-talking night at our Eden place.

But, first, we must have spring.
Your Martha

# BOOK TWO

# SPRING

"If I keep a green bough in my heart,
then the singing bird will come."
—Chinese proverb

## 17 March 2013 — 8:22 A.M.

Dearest Brian,

The only time I feel whole—completely myself—is when I am, pen in hand, writing you another letter. The soft slur of ink as it washes across page after page, filling the emptiness with writing, and the solace of the pages in this particular journal (so much thicker than the last one) that are waiting to pull me through the spring and summer and early fall. I find you here, more heart-breakingly visceral than anywhere else I try to seek you out. This is why I return every day, sifting through a lifetime of moments to stand in the still pool of your love—safe, supported and held by beauty, by you.

## 2:06 P.M.

My darling,

When you were alive and I could hear you down in the kitchen, as, perhaps, I was resting, reading on our bed on a Sunday afternoon (when all was normal), I could drift in the noises of the house. Hear the cupboard door open and close gently (you were a graceful and gentle-moving man), know that you had pulled out a red mug, and that the kettle, brought not quite to a boil, would be lifted from its base, a small perfect triangular gauze bag of green tea would slip into the cup, and the water poured over it would be allowed to steep in the spring-coloured essence for thirty seconds, exactly. Then, discarding the bag, you would lean, all the lean six-foot-six inches of you, back against the counter, lift the cup in your left hand—as we are both left-handed—and slowly sip the burning liquid. How could you drink something so hot? Hotter than these tears that flow down my face.

xo M.

18 March 2013 — 8:26 A.M.

Brian,

I've decided not to take sorrow to bed with me and, for the most part, write these letters in the morning. The idea is that I might sleep better. I'm not sure that it'll work. Last night, last time I checked the clock it was 3:36 A.M. This morning, as a point of edification (on the Grief Train), I'm feeling all over sore, as a part of sore—ow.

Between wakefulness and slumber we had a conversation in which you said to me, "Take this time for you. It's yours to spend with writing and music. Don't worry about me—I'm here, as always, supporting you. Be grateful for your health and for this opportunity, do it well, but be tender with yourself, Martha, don't go overboard."

Later, in a dream, I was in the kitchen and you came back from the store, up the stairs, carrying two bags of groceries. It was a hot day. Your lovely long bare arms were tanned and you were wearing your pink t-shirt—same shade of pink as the rose quartz heart Kirsten wrapped for me in silver. I wear it, sometimes, on a chain that resembles a fishing line. And after all, I am—especially these days—a fisher of dreams.

You set down the bags and came to me, reaching out to lightly sweep my hair off my shoulders, and then you bent and kissed me, again and again, my lips, my face, my neck, and after that you held me to you just so against your heart, and rocked me in the bigness of your arms.

You have ruined me, honey, for short men.

All my love,
M.

19 March 2013 — 9:46 A.M.

Darling,

You were in my dreams, it seemed, for the entire night. In one of the dreams we were at the cottage—though in the way of dreams it looked different. A small car pulled up the driveway—an under-age driver of around fourteen and his brother who looked to be around eight. The little brother was sent to ask us for our valuables. We invited him into our living space and you proceeded to make friends with him.

You produced a pot, actually a large vessel, of honey-coloured holy oil. You lit a flame and then instructed him to sit with you and to do so in quiet and grateful contemplation. Which you both did. He was adorable. His brother kept looking in the windows, hands in his pockets, cooling his heels while all this was going on, lurching around impatiently.

I don't recall how the dream ended. By all thought processes, having robbers come to your door is a nightmare. On some levels it was. The sense of invasion, albeit surprising in its outcome.

Our lives were invaded when you died—the surprise of it a psychic burning. But this morning I am left to ponder the beautiful child thief and my beautiful spiritual husband, heads bent in prayerful contemplation over a glowing bowl of honey-sweet fire. Amen, my darling.

All my love,
Martha


Later — 3:31 P.M.

Darling,

You would think that reissuing Myra's dog licence from your name to mine wouldn't be difficult. Except, of course, you have to tell the reason for the change. I told them that you'd died—a

71

reasonable reason. Then they wanted a letter to that effect and out loud I said to the perfectly nice person on the other end of the line, "No thank you," and thought, "Fuck you," and so Myra still belongs to you, a dead man, and it's just one of the many daily things about being a widow that no one other than another widow would recognize. She would think it perfectly understandable that I got off the phone and burst into tears. Later, she would nod her head in recognition as, while tackling our taxes, I tenderly pored over your Pharmacare receipts, noting that one of your prescriptions was issued on the day of our forty-fifth wedding anniversary (no more anniversaries). I didn't quite do all that was required of our tax work, today. I could feel you, hand on my back, saying, "This doesn't have to be done all at once. Tackle a little bit, a day at a time, and pretty soon it'll be out of your hair."

So I went out and bought dog food. The bags are getting smaller. The price was outrageous.

But the sun was shining, the air smelled as sweet as spring, and March is almost over. The mountain ash outside the window of your office, where I now do all my creative work, shivers, lightly wind-tossed, against a brilliant blue sky. Long ago, when you planted it, it was only about six feet tall and now it reaches past this second-storey eagle's eye view of the world.

xo M.

## 24 March 2013 — 8:19 A.M.

My darling Brian,

On my way home from a visit to Eden/Ninette yesterday, in the late afternoon, a bald eagle flew across the highway, tipped his left wing and then flew off into a sky that was, after a dull, cold day, starting to turn to the tender blue of spring.

On Friday, around suppertime, I'd called our friend Marilyn and she was, for all kinds of reasons, feeling poorly. For one, her beloved grandcat, "The Prince," had just died. I got off the phone, dashed through dinner, called her at 6:00 and asked if she'd like a little company. Well, she sure would. Hopped into Rabbit after throwing a few things into a bag and was on those country roads by 6:15. I arrived at around 8:30—this new car sure is peppy, honey—and there was Marilyn, throwing open her front door to me, all smiles, and her two-word greeting, as always, "Girl Friend!"

We drank wine and ate chips with her homemade salsa and got slightly blitzed and cried and reminisced and fell, generally, into the joy of simply being together. We both had the best sleep, woke refreshed, sat around and had breakfast and drank coffee and watched the birds and the deer. ("Poor buggers are starving—my nephew's bringing over a big bag of feed for them, later.") If you remember, the deer come up on her front deck and make a helluva mess, tossing seeds everywhere, and she loves every moment of it. Yesterday, there was a large flock of redpolls at her feeders—tiny lively birds with flashes of downy reddish-pink. Unlike some, they fly even further north of us for the summer months, returning every winter to remind us that there is life in the snow.

And there is life in friendship. Life in two kindred spirits simply minding the day and holding each other's hearts.

All my love,
M.


## 25 March 2013—2:52 P.M.

Oh my darling,

Should anyone get the idea, the hopeful idea, that there is an end to sorrow, they'd be wrong. Sorrow can go down deep, lurking like some creature at the bottom of things—all it takes is running into one or two people who don't know you've died and it surfaces, comes looking for me and pulls me under again. I suppose it's the measure of a man when there isn't a single person I tell, who knew you, who doesn't either tear up or burst into tears. Partly, I think, people loved us as a couple, found our deep connection inspiring, and can't stand to think that we are no longer walking around in the world as one.

I'm not sure how we got this way in everyone's mind's eye. Early in our marriage we had dips just like everyone else, working things out the way good couples do. But something wonderful happened when you closed the doors of your office in 2000 and stayed home with me. We grew ever closer and midway through the decade fell headlong back into lovely lusty love—even better than the first time around. Took us both by surprise, dear God, and we were smart enough to take the year off, to be available to each other and unavailable to everyone else. There was no necessity to "work" at things, we knew each other so well, we read each other's thoughts and lived for each other and took joy in each other. When I got sick in 2007 we readjusted and pulled together all the more fiercely. When asked, all in all, why it worked, how it worked, we trotted out words like "respect" and "compassion," but really how a couple gets that close is part mystery, part luck, and maybe the rest is karma.

I, too, hate the thought of you no longer being in the world. But your loss, for me, is an inescapable daily occurrence, sometimes shocking, sometimes tender, sometimes full of wonder, and always backlighting my every gesture, my very heartbeat with the slow sad progress of the days and months since you left me.

All my love,
M.


## 27 March 2013—10:20 A.M.

Dearest Brian,

Four months since you left us.

Heard from your/our dear friend Nancy. At your funeral we

read what she'd written: "We worked together for twenty years. When we moved [your public relations and advertising firm] from Border Place to Albert Street there was street life, jazz concerts in Market Square, shops and art galleries to visit during lunch hour. Usually we ate our respective lunches in the office: my V8, soup and fruit, and your homemade granola and apple with tea. We read our copies of *MacWorld* and discussed everything: software, ethics, movies, and the meaning of life. Everything but sports."

Ah, yes, absolutely everything but sports—that would be the case. Whenever you and I watched TV there was never a conflict with the remote. We headed straight for *Nova* and *The Passionate Eye* and *Independent Lens* and, fingers crossed, PBS was not showing *Lawrence Welk.*

You were not a man whose preferences ran to gratuitous violence, car chases, boys' nights out, beer and steaks. Well, sometimes beer if it was from a microbrewery, but certainly not (in the last several years) steak or, for that matter, as you so poignantly put it after driving behind a pig truck for several miles one summer, "Anything that once had eyes."

Your favourite book of 2009 was a Christmas present from Kirsten and Mike—a tome called *The Bloodless Revolution—A Cultural History of Vegetarianism from 1600 to Modern Times,* by Tristram Stuart. You plowed through it with relish, it was a hard read, but your brilliance at that point was intact.

Golf, religious fervour, hunting and guns made your eyes glaze over. You prized honesty and simplicity and authenticity. Cheap laughs left you somewhat baffled—probably because your own sense of humour was so original and dry. And everyone who dreams about you has such a specific vision of a man who was creative and practical—a winning combination.

In her email to me Nancy also said, "I recently had a Brian dream—very simple. It seemed so real. I was at your place, I'd come to ask Brian how to do something with my camera. He explained it carefully (whatever it was) and all was well. You brought coffee and we talked for a while—and I woke happily."

Our friend Pat Farrell said to me a while ago, "Brian isn't simply appearing in our dreams randomly. He actually is in our dreams. There's a difference."

Well, yes, I believe it. You are a free agent, now. Rock on, gentle spirit.

With all my love,
M.

## Good Friday, 29 March 2013 — 8:07 A.M.

Darling,

I've gone through entire days lately where I'm fine, but then suddenly I'm not. Such is the chilly continent of grief. "Spring Will be a Little Late This Year"—that's the weather report from my heart.

But if anyone were to ask me—what do you do with sorrow?—I'd say do, during the day, at least one thing that you love, do give yourself that gift. Like me, here and now, watching the steady wash of words flow out of my icy places, warming me, thawing me, because I love to write and I love to write to you, honey, and the very thought of you makes me hope for spring. And hope, as you and I often said, is so important. Sometimes hope is all we have.

Loving you with April in my heart,
Martha

## Later, 11:00 A.M.

Kirsten just got off the phone with somebody who'd said, "So your mom's doing okay, right?"

Kirsten went on a rant to me, "Why do people want to speed

you through the darkness? I wanted to say, 'No, she's not doing all right. She didn't break her leg. She lost her soulmate and partner of forty-nine years. She's not okay. Will she be okay? Yes, at some point maybe. But after four months? No. She's absolutely not okay.' Stuff just drops out of people's mouths like garbage cans."

## 31 March 2013 – 8:17 A.M.

Brian honey,

Easter Sunday. The sun is shining, the snow is still with us. Yesterday I accomplished two things—a walk with the dog down the back alley and a slow fixated construction of a grant application. In the application I quite rightly was requested to defend my proposal, which is for a memoir called "Letters to Brian." As I am writing this, all kinds of moments with you sift through my head. When you were sick, every morning around this time I'd wake you up to give you a mild dose of an anti psychotic—but is any of that type of drug mild, especially when taken for a year? You never complained. You'd wake up, take the little pill I'd given you, slap it into your mouth with your big gentle hand and drift off to sleep again. I remember at the lake, especially, how big your hand looked against your face—those long elegant fingers in the shadows of the room.

Yesterday, Kirsten said to me, "I know that in your head you're telling yourself that you have all kinds of things to live for. You go along, you do stuff and so on. But this is grief, and in your heart you still don't actually feel like being here. So it's your heart you've got to fix."

So, okay, maybe it's time to go and talk to somebody, honey. Maybe she's right. Maybe I can't do this alone.

Sorrow.

All my love,
Martha

## Later, 11:40 A.M.

Going for a walk in the woods is not the ultimate cure for grief, but it's a pretty comfortable band-aid. Allan, your brother, said, when he called to arrange a time to meet with our dogs at Assiniboine Forest, "You don't sound exactly one hundred percent."

"You'd be right about that," I told him.

However, fresh air, sunshine, sky an eye-popping blue—Rembrandt could not have done a better job—and I said, "Well, thank you as usual for this."

"Glad it helped," Al said, as we went our separate ways.

## Tuesday 2 April 2013—3:32 P.M.

My darling Brian,

Yesterday I didn't write to you because I was having a hard time doing anything. It's the old up and down—one day things feel okay, the next you're flat on your ass. That's not complicated to figure out. As our wise daughter, the healer, says: it's grief. Yup, this is what it looks like.

Today, I made an appointment to speak to a grief counsellor who has, among other things, worked as a United Church minister and as the Provincial Spiritual Health Coordinator. In another incarnation she has been a well-known teacher and spiritual renegade and all-around visionary. In yet another lifetime, she was a journalist. In other words, she's my kind of person. You used to read her faith column in the *Winnipeg Free Press* and would often remark, "Karen Toole is one of the few people who can make sense of it all."

When I called she remembered an encouraging email I'd sent when she was still writing for the paper. It was one of those moments in her life when she needed a little shot in the arm, I delivered it, and she's remembered it to this day.

Anyway, she's a gem. We spoke for about twenty minutes over

the phone and in that short time I felt that, finally, I was not alone; that somebody outside of a handful of people could make sense of it all.

"What you are going through is absolutely normal—you feel terrible. Just know that four months is a very short time," she told me, "and believe it or not that's just about the mark when people start asking for help."

She understood, immediately, how close we'd been and said, "Not everybody is going to get that—how deep this loss is for you."

When Kirsten and Mike got home from work today and asked how I was I joked, "I'm a weather report. Variably cloudy with scattered showers."

Widows, as well as widowers, I think, need help. There comes a time when in spite of doing everything right—not turning to the bottle for solace, finding meaningful connections with friends and family, doing meaningful work, getting the hands-on solace of massages, doing yoga, getting fresh air and sunshine, being spontaneous and so on, simply isn't enough. Comes a time when you need an alternately dispassionate and compassionate ear. I'll keep you posted, honey. I'm seeing her on Monday.

All my love,
Martha


## Wednesday 3 April 2013—3:25 P.M.

Darling,

The value of writing these letters to you, partly as a way of "seeing" my journey, is that I can look back, go back. In a letter to you on the 25th of March, for instance, I told you about giving the news of your death to people who'd cared about you and didn't know you were gone. I realize now, even more keenly than I did a few days ago, just how hard it was to do that. I'm also beginning to see a pattern for grief that makes me feel less alone. Just the fact that I'm going to be talking to a person who hears people's stories all the time puts a normal spin on it. Grief is a journey that everyone, at some point, must take.

So I was calm doing our taxes today, washing dishes, cleaning up after the dog, making much needed appointments and doing some preliminary and quite joyful research on the lyricist Sammy Cahn, whose lovely songs Jeff and I will be preparing for the Winnipeg Jazz Festival. I did a lot of singing, too, as I cleared out the various piled-up papers that are lying about the house. In other words, I've found a bit of energy.

While I was doing all this I thought about how, unlike a broken leg, a broken heart is so tricky to mend—one band-aid at a time.

In the cleanup, I came across an email that I'd printed and kept. In it I was discussing with Glenn Buhr (my then go-to piano guy and all around musical director) various ideas for a concert that he and I were going to do, throwing song ideas back and forth. In a p.s. to him I said, "Brian just bought me the Leonard Cohen concert album. He mentioned to me in his usual mad genius manner that "Closing Time" would be a fabulous closing number for us—done with audience participation. I keep giggling, imagining it—would we distribute song sheets?"

## Next morning, 4 April—8:53 P.M.

Darling,

So okay, we never did do "Closing Time," however we did successfully tackle, at your nudging, Patricia Barber's hypnotic, and out there, "The Moon," and if you'll recall, by gum, it was a show-stopper. Likewise, I've absolutely loved performing Barber's "If I Were Blue"—all pretty much rubato with its hinted-at Latin feel. Jeff and Steve Hamilton and I explored both of those songs at the Jazz Festival a couple of years ago and people were mesmerized.

You always said, "Don't give them the same old—bring them

along with something new. If you are connecting with them, they'll stay right with you."

How right you were. You were so involved with the music, nudging me with ideas that felt as if I were being led off the map. Over the years I got up the courage to perform, among others, Barber's "Dansons la Gigue," and "Gotcha" and "Pieces"—various of my musicians jumping into them all with a "what the hell, if we fall off the planet we'll do it together" attitude that proved exhilarating.

You were right behind me when Knut Haugsoen and I did an evening with the Winnipeg Symphony. When that opportunity arose right after our CD *Change of Heart* won the Prairie Music Award for Outstanding Jazz Album, I said to you, "Dear God, what do I think I'm doing?"

"You're singing with a symphony orchestra," you said with a chuckle. "How many singers get the opportunity to sing in a concert hall, backed by an entire symphony?" When the rehearsal with the orchestra came—a mere two hours for the whole evening (how the hell did that work?), I was just about peeing myself.

And then it was time for the concert, you departing for the audience, me departing for the green room. "Just go out there and enjoy it," you told me before you gave me a quick hug. "Think about being inside the evening and connecting the way you do so well with an audience."

From the green room, Knut and Kelly Marques and Steve Hamilton and I heard the overture to *Man of La Mancha*, right up to the place where he dreamed the impossible, and then I went out on stage with my bandmates and the full symphony and began the impossible concert. But from Steve's opening walking bass line of "Deed I Do" to the closing "No More Blues," when the audience requested an encore, it was sheer delight—a love fest.

Afterwards, all smiles, bursting your buttons, you said, "You looked great up there. You sounded great."

Later, My Maureen said to me, "You looked so relaxed up there."

I should have told her, "With Brian's steady-as-she-goes prompting."

I was nineteen years old when I met you in the fall of 1963. By the following spring I was to perform in my (then) coloratura soprano voice for the music festival in the old Winnipeg Auditorium. You were my boyfriend down in the audience as I went up on that stage and sang "O Mio Babbino Caro," so nervous that my knees actually knocked together. The whole thing, to my mind at least, was a mess. I came off stage mortified and ran out into the street.

You came after me—you were so tall those long legs didn't take any time at all to catch up. You reached out and stopped me, turned me around, caught my face in your hands as I was falling apart in front of you, and said, "You have to go back in there. It wasn't as terrible a performance as you think it was. Come on back inside and hear what the adjudicator has to say."

You were twenty years old. Such a wise twenty-year-old. For the next almost fifty years you kept right on doing things like that, supporting me, picking me up, finding and saying the right words.

All my love,
Martha

"EACH GRIEF IS SHAPED DIFFERENTLY."

—KAREN TOOLE

## 10 April 2013

My darling Brian,

It's been a few days since I've written. On Monday I went to see the wonderful Karen Toole for what turned out to be a most helpful and healing session of grief counselling. Took in our photo, that one taken by Our Maureen in the summer of 2007 under a canopy of trees in city park, me tucked against you just so. Karen looked at it and said, "I feel as if I know him and he's what I expected. You two are a really good fit and I mean that on the deepest level. Few people are lucky enough to be married to their soulmate. And yet that means that the immensity and intensity of your grief is vast and deep."

She went on to say, "Each grief is shaped differently, which is why grief groups don't always work—the people in them don't feel they're being understood. With people who have lost a spouse, for instance, you have everything from soulmates right through to marriages where people have fallen out of love, maybe don't even like each other any more, barely tolerate each other, go out for dinner and see people, but basically the marriage is a sham. It's hard on those people, too, because everyone has certain expectations about how they should be feeling and that can make them feel guilty."

I shared some dreams about you with her, mine and other people's, and she said, "Brian is a joyful spirit now. He's free. So he can afford to be present."

She didn't for a minute make me feel that I was goofy to give voice to what I'm beginning to understand as "you on a different plane." In many ways she validated it—you may have checked out but you keep checking back in.

I ran into our neighbour Betty Iris today, nun and heart healer. She's in her eighties, as you know, and I love her to pieces. She hugged me and said, "How are you doing?"

"Lots of ups and downs."

"So are people telling you to get on with it? Get over it?"

"Not in so many words."

"They'll think things like that anyway, not really meaning to but they want you to move on."

Aided by both her no-nonsense concern and Karen's, I thought, "But that's not realistic."

Betty Iris went on, "It'll take three years, at least, maybe for-ever. Don't let them rush you. It's been what, four—five months?"

Karen had said, "It's very soon, only four months or so and that's really not very long."

"You're seeing Karen Toole?" Betty Iris said, her eyes widen-ing. "She's wonderful!"

"Yes, she is," I said, and thought, "So are you."

Sat all evening inside your orange fleece, watching nature pro-grams on TV. Somewhere during that time I said out loud to you, "Darling, you are welcome to just simply come inside and inhabit my body. We're twinned, anyway."

You did. And we are.

All my love,
M.


## 11 April 2013

Darling,

This letter to you is entitled: Wearing Brian.

Whenever I'm feeling Lost and Alone, which is a lot of the time, I wear you. Nothing like lifting my arms, putting my hands through your sleeves, easing you over my head and having you drift down my body. Your soft orange L.L. Bean fleece (you were so tall that everything you owned had to be special-ordered) is a favourite and so, recently, is the red and beige and grey sweater that, like the fleece, weighs almost nothing and was knitted for you by your mother about twenty years ago. The body length fits me like a dress; the sleeves, even rolled up, hang halfway down my hands. Warmly inside you, surrounded by your energy, I write or simply mind the day.

I would recommend this to anyone who has lost a beloved spouse—although, admittedly, while it would probably work effortlessly for most women, it might not be quite so easy for most men. I'm not sure, for instance, what a very large man would do with a small lacy sweater, but then grief is inventive.

When I am Wearing Brian, my heart is a little less sore, my daily decisions are a little less wacky and I feel more myself—which is to say, more like the equation of two rather than the lonely number of one. I can just be and drift and feel calm the way I did whenever your arms came around me.

My love xox M.

## 13 April 2013

Darling, got an email this morning from Jeff. The subject was: Jazz Festival Surprise. The message: "Hi Martha! Patricia Barber's gonna be in Winnipeg and it's not on our night (the night of our performance)—means we can go! J."

I quickly sent off, "Yes! Want to go with me?"

He shot back, "Let's go, but don't buy a ticket yet. I may have a pass."

An hour later I got an email from your/our friend, Nancy: "I'm sure that Brian would be tickled to know that you and Patricia Barber, his favourite singers, will both be performing at the Jazz Festival!"

I remember one time when you were reading Barber's blog. You connected with this woman's music so deeply that you were also tickled to discover that she, like us, had an Airedale Terrier (an unusual choice of dog) and that her partner's name is Martha (in my lifetime I've actually met very few Marthas).

All of this feels orchestrated as usual by you, honey, or at the very least oddly synchronous. I so wish that you were here, physically. And now I'm a faucet again. But bravely forth, my dearest darling, with new wings on my heart.

My love, love, love—
your Martha

15 April 2013 — 4:47 P.M.

Darling,

Tonight I'm improvising a tofu dish with strained tomatoes and basil pesto, something I think you would have loved. As well I'm testing a new product—a sprouted rice blend of red and brown and wild rice with quinoa which I know you would have added, with all of your enthusiasm and sweet curiosity, to your own cooking. This is a small robbery of memory. But, still, it stings—memories such as this gave borders to our days.

Every day I kiss your picture on the refrigerator, leaning in to give it several good smacks, five to be precise, seven when I'm noticing more fully the image I chose—you staring at the camera with one eye skillfully crossed. God, you were goofy. Fittingly, the photo has become increasingly smeared and smells of peanut butter and coffee from several long months of not being able to kiss you, the real thing. As an aside, your eyes were a rich dark brown. God, you were handsome.

I remember the first time I saw you, October, 1963. You were sitting in front of me in math class.

You were back in school after being away for a couple of years (your dad's death, your best friend Derry's death, your surrogate father's death, all that charming stuff) and were upgrading your courses in preparation for a business administration diploma. I was lumping along, after a great deal of childhood ill health and the chest surgery, when I was eighteen, that was finally helping me get a leg up on life. So there I was trying to finish up grade twelve math. I didn't know then how grateful I would later be for my abject stupidity in the subject. We would never have met, otherwise. No wonder I still find messages from you in the synchronous—they've been brilliantly there right from the start.

Anyway, it was the back of your head I saw first—a head of clean shiny curly black hair. I wanted to touch it. I hadn't even seen your face, and yet, like a deep bell sounding, I thought, "This is the man I'm going to marry."

Then you turned around—a face full of freckles—and did a double take. As class ended we talked and apparently I blathered away while you landed on the clue that I was living on Niagara Street off Grant.

You lived one street over on Waterloo, way to hell and gone in the other direction, and had no idea of my house number. And so next morning there was Annabelle, the family friend with whom I was staying, at the front door, trying to hurry me out to catch my bus as she said, "There's this little red Triumph that keeps going around the block and here he comes again."

I leapt out to the sidewalk and you swerved, just missing the curb.

"I was wondering," you said, lurching to a stop, "if you'd like a ride to school."

Years later, I walk with your brother Allan and our dogs, Toby and Myra, at Assiniboine Forest just about every Sunday. Last Sunday Al told me about how he and Toby had come across a dead deer in the forest a couple of weeks ago.

"A young one," he said, "still untouched by anything, so obviously it hadn't been dead long. Anyway, you know how Toby loves tracking deer, but he was so respectful of this one, going around, sniffing at it, then he walked away and just stayed beside me. I don't want to read too much into it but he seemed ..."

"Wistful?"

"Yeah. Kind of thoughtful for some time. Dogs are amazing animals."

After a while we came to a winter meadow. The light on the snow and delicate plants reminded me of how you looked at landscape—with a photographer's eye—and some of your photos are breathtaking. Allan, your photographer brother, told me about how the light had been so interesting the other day in that particular area.

"It just glowed," he said.

"All about the play of light in photography," I added, "light and shadow."

"That's right."

He carries an indelible piece of you—all about the beauty of light and shadow and how it plays with our lives.

Yesterday morning, another Sunday, he had an unexpected meeting, so I went to the dog park with Myra, as a spur-of-the-moment thing, and found you in somebody else.

Our old dog park friend, Bill Barker, who has not been to Fields of Fido for three years because one of his dogs was injured there, was walking around with Logan and Megan. He told me about his new happier life in retirement and how his health had improved. I told him that I was thrilled for him—he's the same age you were when you took your own retirement. Bill and his wife, Dianne, are soulmates—there seem to be more couples like that than I previously thought—and she must be so grateful for his new healthy life.

"I used to be so negative," he said, as we circled the park, "but now I'm not."

He knew you had gone and said that he and Dianne were so very sorry. Last time we saw them was this time last year, and he gave us that link for a new laser therapy treatment for glioblastoma that was being developed in the States.

At the end of our walk, he put his arms around me and said, "You took care of Brian and now he's taking care of you. He still has his arms around you—just like this, believe it. He has your back. Listen, there are no accidents. We met today for a reason."

It was such a lovely moment. It did make me feel lonely for you, however. I came home to Kirsten and Mike and wept and wept and our six-foot-tall goddess of a daughter wrapped me up in yet another embrace and Mike made us his Sunday morning pancakes.

I will always run into people who knew you—the Before Brian

and After Brian moments that are so unavoidably wrenching. I miss you so much and, dear God, it's snowing again. Will this winter never end?

All my love—
M.

## 16 April 2013 — 7:52 A.M.

Dearest Brian,

Just brought my breakfast tray into your office. Am now at your desk, while the food cools, and I'm moved to write you another letter. As I walked into the room and set down the tray I looked out the window at a very grey day and thought, "What would Brian be thinking right now if the tables were turned—if it were me almost five months dead and him left beginning again without me?"

Your answer quickly came: "Yes, I would be sad. Yes, I would feel lonely, but I would also be looking around for things to do with the rest of my life. I'd probably work on this unfinished house while I was figuring it all out, and then when that was all done I'd sell the place and move on. Along the way I'd probably also check out courses in architecture, go to art shows, maybe start going to the Yoga Centre. And, Martha, I'd likely start looking for a girlfriend. I used to say to you that people are going to start living longer, a lot longer, and there'll be a need to live well and find some real enjoyment with that extra time. I was healthy, other than this thing growing in my head, and I envisioned a future that was filled with the contentment of just being with you. Did I love you? Oh, yes. We were hip-to-hip. I loved touching you everywhere. And while I was alive, especially when I was sick, I wanted you constantly in my sight. I couldn't get enough of looking at you and the world I was leaving. But if it were me left behind, in spite of how deep my emotions ran for you—and, yes, there's nobody like you—I'd still look for somebody. Don't close yourself off to that possibility."

Seems you've just written me a letter, honey—all you'd have to do is sign it! Thanks for opening your voice to me, what a gift! It's your voice I want, not the boyfriend.

My love,
Martha

18 April 2013—9:36 A.M.

Brian, I've just put in a few long days to get together an arts grant proposal for a manuscript called "Letters to Brian"—selected letters from all this writing I've been doing to keep you with me, somehow. I still can't process your loss and as I culled through about a hundred and forty pages (I'm probably underestimating, here) of handwritten letters to you, it wasn't enough to help me wrap my head around the fact that you've slipped past my touch.

My spirited ninety-one-year-old cousin, Agnes (work-out-three-times-a-week Agnes) just lost her husband of sixty-seven years. She said she'll need to talk to me because I've been so recently through it, and, she says, "I don't know how to handle it, really."

Agnes is also wise enough to understand that none of us knows, really—this in spite of the fact that I'm starting to feel like a walking authority. I don't know—maybe I can help somebody with these letters to you. But the overarching reason I'm writing them remains: I love you and miss you and want you and hold you in aching and tender and ever hopeful memory. I desire to move you past the barrier of death and into another realm of experiencing you. It's a trick I'm learning to do. Are you behind my eyes, now, as I'm writing this? Please let that be the case, my lovely lovely man.

Your Martha

## Friday 19 April 2013 — 7:52 A.M.

Brian honey,

"Death is part of life." How often do I hear that old saw being dragged out—and of course it's because words truly do fail people. One of the most significantly transforming experiences of a person's life is the loss of someone so dear to them that they can't find a place for their grief and can't wrap their heads around the notion of the world going on without their beloved.

"Very few people," my grief counsellor, Karen, said to me, "are ready to be told that it's an opportunity for change. A lot of people want to smack me when I tell them that."

"But what you're saying to me—and I get it—is that grief is transformative."

"Exactly."

It's been about two weeks since we had that discussion, Brian, and that particular idea has been working on me, just as she hoped it would.

I'm no stranger to reinvention. And neither are you. We moved through being a young dating couple to being a young married couple and then to being parents. I was a completely besotted stay-at-home mom. I'd been a secretary (to support my art) for seven years and had, for the most part, deeply disliked it. But being at home with our baby on my hip, suddenly pets—a dog and a cat—pears, in September, glowing up at me from a blond wood kitchen chopping block, a neighbourhood of laughing, chaotic life spent under the outspreading arms of river elms, and I was in heaven. Baking bread, playing with and singing to our daughter, family outings, the beginnings of my first novel—for me, especially, that was a time of deep contentment.

But then we switched gears again and you went from being a stockbroker, which *you* disliked, to a business in the country with a man who'd invented a machine to pick up round hay bales—in the early days of round hay bales. I had grown up in the country and so knew intimately its joys but also the (sometimes) insular mindsets of its people. So, somewhat reluctantly, I went along with it, finding a big yellow farmhouse to rent, "The Prairie Canary," and we moved from the city to the country and my initial concerns evaporated. We now had a curious three-year-old daughter, a dog, two cats, three or four rabbits, a truck, wonderful neighbours who became best friends, city friends and family who couldn't stay away from the place and who would arrive as early as possible on Friday and leave as late as possible on Sunday.

We were there four years. Midway through you started to do a lot of travelling for your work. This was the mid-seventies and a revolution was underway for women and their baffled husbands— no less so in the country. Roles began to shift, and you were married to a feisty person who was feeling very much as if you thought what she did wasn't important and what you did was. I was resentful and lonely, and one time when you came back after yet another week on the road—we were in the truck on our way to pick up Kirsten from a sleepover with her friend Jodi—I turned to you and said, "Well, I'm taking Kirsten away with me next week to visit Mom and Dad in the city and I'm not sure how long we'll be gone." This fell out of my mouth almost as I was thinking it. I think your jaw literally dropped. You hadn't a clue what was coming.

I went on, "I have no idea what you'll do here all by yourself, but maybe you'll get a better grip on just how pissed off I am."

You said, slowing the truck, looking at the road, at me, back at the road, "Are you telling me you want a *divorce*?"

What a ridiculous idea. It made me even more furious. "What I am saying," I said, "is I want you to wake up and smell the coffee!"

Like any man who is brought to his knees in terror by the woman he loves, you did the thing that most quickly came to mind—a family trip. I was given air tickets very shortly after that, on Mother's Day, for you and Kirsten and me to go to Disneyland. It was a wonderful trip—but for the rest of our married lives

I would check in, periodically, acting on a piece of advice I'd been given earlier in the decade.

A Gypsy fortuneteller told me, "You are married to a man who loves you but once in a while you'll need to throw cold water on him." She was an early feminist—probably started her own revolution. Hundreds of women went around in the seventies following that woman's advice. She's either a very old lady by now or has gone on to her own just reward—checking in periodically with neighbours and family and friends, close to their ears with the gift of an idea that is endlessly practical and transformative and renewable.

And so here I am transformed by the chill of grief—a gift I never expected—and that you never wanted me to have in all your tender love for me as we grew as a couple, ever tighter, ever more fiercely protective of each other and the life together that we both knew would someday end.

The last year of your life can be marked by asides to people, out of my earshot, where you fretted about how I would do after you were gone. But I'm doing, and becoming, and growing, and somewhere in all of this I sense your own growth. I do believe that spirits grow, free to do that, just as you seem to be free to help me see this new life I'm living.

All my love,
Martha

"ALL GRIEF IS DIFFERENT, SOME SITS AT THE SURFACE, SOME GOES DOWN MANY LAYERS."

—KAREN TOOLE

## Tuesday, 23 April 2013—5:43 P.M.

Well, darling, I threw my hat into the ring—the slender version of "Letters to Brian" is off to the granting body at the Manitoba

Arts Council, fingers crossed. Meantime I continue these letters to you—some I'll share with the world, some I won't, and that way we'll still have our own current of conversation as I flow to you through the whole of it with all of my heart.

I went to see Karen Toole yesterday and am still processing our talk. As I was leaving she said, "What some people might misconstrue as wallowing in grief—as they look in on something they can't possibly understand unless they've gone through it—is, in actual fact, immersion—which is a very necessary part of grief work."

Love and loss, darling—that's been one of my subjects as a fiction writer for forty years. Well acquainted with the territory from decades of my own writing, a place of understanding of my own losses and trying to understand, at least fictionally, the losses of others.

During our conversation Karen said, "All grief is different, some sits at the surface, some goes down many layers. When you started to talk to me last time about Brian, I kept thinking, 'Please don't take me down another layer, Martha,' and then you'd drop me down a couple more."

But you see it's not an unfamiliar place for me, that darkness, and she confirmed for me that it's a natural and necessary place to go.

She also said, "I've been thinking about Brian since you 'introduced' me to him at our last session. It seems he was a man of courage."

"Oh yes," I said, and burst into tears. "I'm so glad you said that. The way he handled his life and his illness and his death."

"And," she said, "the way you describe him, he was a man who lived in the fulsomeness of his own being. So he could die with grace, let go, nothing left unfinished. There wasn't a lot of ego there."

"All correct."

"He never competed with you."

"God no, never."

94

"That's rare. He didn't compete. He supported."

"Right on both counts," I said, glowing with the happiness of her recognition of you, Brian.

"But how did you, Martha, stay so present, so in the moment with him the year he was ill? Many people would have wanted to hurry along his death because they couldn't stand it, and could not have been so present with him in the day-to-day. So how did you do it?"

I thought about all these letters I've been writing and the refrain that keeps repeating, certainly in our lives in the past dozen or so years, and said, "Gratitude."

She sat back, and said, "Ahhh."

Then I told her the story about how at the time of your diagnosis they put you on steroids and that spun you into a psychotic episode, a mania—you were not yourself, uncharacteristically aggressive and somewhat menacing when things didn't go your way—and this all ended in you being taken by the police just before Christmas to the emergency ward (the only way we could get a psychiatric assessment) and the great searing sorrow of your confusion over that, a good man being taken out of his own house by the police, just as the Mennonite Children's Choir arrived at our door singing "Silent Night." So horrible that on some levels, now, we have to make jokes about it as a family.

Kirsten said to me just before the police arrived, "Mom, get out of here, I don't want you to see this." I said, "I don't want *you* to see this." Her hell-tiger response was, "Get the hell out of here, Mom, I mean it. Go to Uncle Eddie's, Shandra will drive you."

For three weeks, over Christmas, you were in hospital. We visited you for hours every day, trying to keep some essence of you buoyed up inside your craziness. I woke up on January 1st, threw out the old calendar, slapped a new one on the wall, flipped through every single month, said, "2012 is going to be a pretty good year," and went to visit you at the hospital.

Your nurses told me that you had been up wandering the

halls, naked, at midnight—New Year's Eve—and this was viewed by some as further indication that you were still nuts. But then I went into your room and you were so grateful and happy to see me and I to see you. You looked as if you had returned to yourself, back from the insanity and rage that the tumour and the drugs had inflicted on you. The man whose return I had so deeply prayed for was back, I knew it, never for a second doubted it. I knew it was you.

I got onto the bed with you and we held each other for a long time and after about half an hour I said, "Let's go for a walk." We went out into the hall, hip-to-hip, your arm around me, mine around you, and I steered us over to the nursing station. I said to the three people sitting there, who turned to look at us in surprise, "I want you to meet my husband, Brian Brooks. This is the man I married. This is who he is. Remember this. Remember him."

Twelve days later we got you out of there.

Karen said, "What you did was restore his dignity."

"Absolutely," I said. "I kept doing it in countless ways through-out the rest of the year. I was grateful to do it. He did the same for me when I was sick—he was brave for me, then, as I was brave for him now—but gratitude, for us, is the bigger word."

xox M.

## 26 April 2013, Friday—8:48 A.M.

Darling Brian,

Kirsten said something to me the other evening when she and I were driving over to a Thai restaurant on Osborne Street. "Some-day, you are going to climb out of the abyss and you'll never look back. Not that you won't miss him, but the big work of grief will be done."

This morning, as she is in her room getting ready to go to

work, her radio is on and Frank Sinatra is singing, "The Best Is Yet to Come."

It's another message through her from you and I'm so grateful to you both.

I am also grateful for your continuous silky stream of messages. *Butterfly Touches* was the title of a painting we saw a few years ago in Reykjavik. It was an image of two souls in human form flying together in some heavenly plane and it so moved you that you would sometimes say, touching me, "Butterfly Touches." I believe in you, in your butterfly touches, in how you continuously touch down and connect with me. I absolutely have to have that— waking up inside a moment, no proof that it is you any more than there is proof of God, but it is an absolute truth for me. And those who can't see it, who haven't had the privilege of being touched by this kind of mystery are, temporarily at least, beyond my window of caring.

Ah, but connection—there I could offer something tangible for the non-believers. Connection was standing yesterday in a fine-art framing store in the Exchange District, a place you and I have been to, the place our friend Pauline chose and you would have chosen for the framing of your painterly photograph—blown up by brother Allan on gorgeous stock to 30 x 25—*Round Hay Bales and Trees in October*—and Pauline and I standing there with Rod Suzuki as we discussed with him the framing, the framing which is her gift to me. The image is breathtaking, honey. When Alice and Eddie and I spread it out to look at a while ago, we said that very word almost in unison, and then one of us said, "It's very French Impressionist." When I told Rod that he looked up from your photo and said, "I was just thinking the same thing, we framed a Monet this morning."

He chose a soft silver frame because he said, "It has presence," echoing what you had said to me when you wanted, a couple of years ago, "something with presence" for our living room. I watched Rod work his delicate discerning eye over the entire image, continuing those echoes of you, approaching the whole thing with exquisite care and tender intelligence.

Once again, I met you in someone else. Ah, yes, mystery.

All my love,
Martha


26 April 2013 — 11:46 P.M.

Darling,

I was at Margaret and Brian MacKinnon's for supper tonight and had the opportunity to read Margaret some of these letters. Just before I left she said she felt you had been there with us all evening.

I had been feeling comfortable the whole time, partly of course because they are such good friends and loved you so dearly, but also, as I told them, I'm getting to the point after five months where I feel less anxious about your physical form not being here and can often just wrap myself up in your essence. There are times in the day where I'll say to myself, "What's that feeling?" and then realize as peace slips around me, "It's Brian." When you were alive you had that effect on me, you would walk into a room, or I'd catch sight of you if we were out somewhere, and there was a moment where I'd take a breath, feel calmer, and then go on with whatever I was doing. So this is what you are doing now, and this is how it feels in my own spirit to have you here. This is you. This is us.

My love,
Martha


27 April 2013 — 8:47 A.M.

My darling Brian,

Five months—an anniversary of sorts. The snow is finally

melting away. What a long cold hard winter it has been. But I'm thinking now of the lake—in about three weeks' time I'll likely be able to open the cottage and be there until late fall, as you and I have done for years. I'll be okay. I'm stronger than I was. I can sometimes go for several hours and feel like my old self, which is to say happy in going about doing whatever it is I'm doing on any given day.

Karen Toole, during our last session, said to me, "I want you to listen when you go out to your lake place this summer."

"Listen?"

"He'll be everywhere out there. He's going to talk to you. All you have to do is open your ears."

I look forward to that, my darling, and I guess I could also say, "Happy anniversary, you joyful spirit."

All of my deep and abiding love,
Martha


## 30 April 2013 – 1:18 P.M.

Darling,

Quite a bit of rain today to green up the world. Snow's almost gone, air smells like spring.

Went with brother Eddie today to talk to a financial advisor at my bank. It was really a good thing to do. The guy, Darryl Choptuik, said, "You shouldn't be kept awake at nights about this," and Eddie added, "Martha has to sleep and not worry about her finances—that would kill her writing." I swear your words dropped out of both their mouths. Everywhere I turn I find you in people's support, in what they say and do, and it fills me with awe.

Today, as I got off the phone with the VISA people, explaining that we'd cut up your credit cards a year and a half ago, I started singing (instead of crying) and it was Sammy Cahn's "Come Fly with Me" with all of its heavenly skyward takeoff. Even though you are flying at times without me, I am finding my own ways to give lift to my (singular) life. Song. Song. Song. Took Myra down the back alley in the rain before breakfast and we were treated to the bubbling melody of a white-throated sparrow—marvellous!

xox Martha

## 1 May 2013—11:42 A.M.

My darling Brian,

Last year on this day at around this time we were loading up the car and making our escape out to the green world of Eden, and a remarkably warm spring. This morning I got out of bed after doing some yoga stretches and looked out the window at a white world and the return, at least temporarily, of Old Man Winter. But I'm singing all the time and it makes me feel good and I just heard from Jeff, who has all the charts ready for us to start experimenting with—sixteen songs. There is such a continued lift in all this music that I barely have the inclination to cry. You seem to slip inside me, inside my song—spirit to spirit—almost anytime of the day. And you travel so light.

All my love,
M.

## 1 May 2013—3:51 P.M.

Well, darling, I was telling My Maureen about how I spent the day of the fifth-month anniversary of your leave-taking. It was at a funeral, Agnes's Hugh's, at the same place (Eirik Bardal's) where we held yours. Alice and Eddie and I went and I was fine, mostly, through the whole thing. I felt you with us.

Of course you were not, by any stretch, a Christian man, and church was always an appalling ordeal for you (you misbehaved and said inappropriate things, and so on) and so at Hughie's funeral we all got to our feet to sing "Onward, Christian Soldiers"—war and Christianity were always a very bad mix for you—and I sang lustily along with everyone else, not paying much attention to the lyrics, until the end of the third verse when I could hear you say, as you had done when you were alive, at someone else's funeral, during a hymn that went on for several verses, "Will this torture never end?" By the end of the fourth verse you said, "That's it, I'm out of here. I'll meet you outside," and then, as you would never have done had you been alive, you got up and left, and the comfort I'd been feeling in having our spirits twinned came to an abrupt end.

It was a lovely service, as funerals go. We stayed around and chatted with everybody and had lunch and then left and went back to Alice and Eddie's for pizza and wine and a movie, but we all felt a little raw, and then I went home (you still weren't back) and cried myself to sleep.

It wasn't until the next day, Sunday, at Beaudry Park, where Myra and I were out walking in God's world under a blue sky with the wind talking in the golden grasses and our feet (mine clad in rubber boots) were splashing along the glistening trails that I felt you move back inside me. Evidently you are still in a position to be offended by things.

xo M.


4 May 2013 — 1:03 P.M.

My darling,

Just listening to the incomparable Shirley Horn singing and playing "Loving You"—with its lyrics about loving, caring, and giving. Isn't that what real love teaches us all? How to give and share and have the whole of a relationship be much larger than the sum of its parts. That's precisely why it takes a lifetime to reach the point where wisdom informs each partner to give a little more here, and share a little more there, and it all falls right in line with respect and compassion—in not making fun of your partner but having fun with him or her, in turning a blind eye to foibles and frailties that are not correctable, in accepting in a loving way the whole person and not judging them in our secret and selfish heart of hearts for what is not quite perfect. Were we lucky? You bet we were. But most especially, were we wise? Yes, a thousand times over. Our marriage vows deepened over time. In good times and in bad. For richer for poorer. In sickness and in health. Until death do us part ... and beyond.

I sit in your office as I write this, the snow has finally gone, the spring birds mostly seem to be back. Last year on this day at the lake, however, we were already greened up by the heavenly weather, grateful to contemplate a stretch of summer even in the face of a very uncertain future. I have photos I took of you on this day wearing your light green fleece, as you went about the yard (Myra tagging along, all happy-dog) pruning bushes and trees and sinking with all your accustomed grace into the loving embrace of spring. All the years we lived out our long life together it was usually you behind the camera, but now you didn't know how to work it anymore. So I took it up and photographed our summer, ever mindful of just what I was recording, and losing.

Most days, now, I feel your joyous free spirit touch down to swirl inside me and lift me up and I believe now that that will continue all this summer long. But forgive me if I take a moment here to feel the long deep stretch of sorrow: I can no longer do something so ordinary as stand behind the camera and continue to capture you as I did for years in my mind's eye. Forty-nine years makes up a lot of moments, darling, but it wasn't, not for me at least, quite the lifetime I wanted to have with you.

My deepest love,
Martha

## 6 May 2013—9:16 A.M.

Brian—

Just called Gerry Paradis and he'll get the water up and running at the cottage for the May long weekend. He says we'll have to keep an eye on the weather, though—the lake is frozen, still! And, of course, most nights it dips to below freezing. It was so nice to just shoot the breeze with him about the weather, the lake levels, which are still kind of low, and about how last year he got his boat in the water by March—"Earliest ever. I wanted to be first to cast off a line and catch a fish."

It all made me smile. You've so often said to me, "You have to continue to connect with people, Martha—it's one of the things you do best."

Before I got off the phone with Gerry I said, "Give your dad my love—and save some for yourself."

He chuckled and said, "Will do."

Connecting with the living is one of the many ways I connect with you. I was talking with Kirsten last night about turning all this letter writing into a memoir and I said, "If you want to still have a relationship with someone who is gone, just how do you go about doing that? How do you reinvent that relationship and what does it look like?"

Our daughter, something of a visionary—like Karen—armed with, among other things, her master's in cultural anthropology, her work as an earth-based healer, and the personal journey that led her to spearhead the first Manitoba Goddess Festival (a radical idea for many) is, as well, a damn fine writer. She's in the throes of writing her own manuscript—a profoundly interesting project that explores the healing and curative powers of the underworld. Grief, she explains, is a journey to the underworld.

"That's really what you're doing—taking that trip. Of course, along the way you're exploring: how do we go about having a relationship with anything that can't be seen? With the Creator, for example."

As you and I are discovering, Brian, this new journey we're on isn't simply about memory—although that is certainly a potent part of it—and while not quite reinventing the wheel, here, it does feels like new territory, and I think we're just getting started.

xo M


"THERE ARE ONLY TWO WAYS TO LIVE YOUR LIFE. ONE IS AS THOUGH NOTHING IS A MIRACLE. THE OTHER IS AS IF EVERY-THING IS."

—ALBERT EINSTEIN

Thursday, 9 May 2013—8:43 A.M.

Darling Brian,

I have just been reading Dr. Eben Alexander's book *Proof of Heaven—A Neurosurgeon's Journey into the Afterlife*. Attacked in 2008 by a rare brain infection that put him in a coma for seven days, Eben Alexander had the ultimate near-death experience which, in and of itself, appears to have made him a revolutionary in the experience of the soul and God and where we go after we transition out of this world into the next.

You had no belief in the existence of God or such a place and neither did he until his own experience. Let me go out on a limb here and say that you know it now, have experienced it all, understand a non-linear transportation of the soul—quantum leaps—where you can be here and there at the same time, and this is why you and I keep connecting in the manner we do.

I remember when you were diagnosed and the mania induced by radiation and steroids filled you with an irrational wild hope and you thought that you were going to live "for another forty years." Then you used as an example my recovery from surgery for breast cancer reconstruction that went so wrong in 2007.

"You died!" you said.

When I told my surgeon sometime after the fact about my own near-death experience, he interrupted me to say, "Martha, it wasn't near-death, you died. You were in the recovery room, you had a massive internal bleed and you flatlined. I can't believe you're standing here in front of me. None of us can. None of us can believe that you're still walking around. It's pretty much a miracle. In fact, it is a miracle."

During my surgery, when twenty-one people worked to save me, I was not in my body. I watched them all down there from the ceiling of the operating room, watched the tops of their heads, felt it best for all concerned that I'd simply remove myself for the time being. I knew that the top of the room was as far as I was going to go, that I was going back eventually and, besides, I was lying in a gorgeous warm brown hand as big as a hammock and as lovely as a day in Heaven, loved, supported. My left arm dangled lazily over the edge of the hand (a right hand) and when I came to, later, that same arm was black and blue and filled with edema and tubed for blood and fluids and medication.

Despite the horrors of that time—the major artery that blew in my abdomen, the seventeen units of blood and blood plasma products, evidence of a great struggle in a body that was fifty percent bruised, an arm swollen to three times its normal size, two days in recovery before I even reached the ICU and then was there, touch and go, for another five days and so on—there was as well for me an element of miracle and profound connection.

After coming back from my clinical death, I was in hospital a total of thirteen days and during that time I lost twenty pounds. As an aside, here, honey, without that game changer I would not have found the strength to deal with losing you. I could have died of a broken heart or driven off a bridge or spun into a suicidal depression. As with any of this stuff, you have to try to make some sense of things, and if you can't do that it's hard to find the will to go on.

Brian, I figure you now know God on some level, just as I touched the Divine cupped in the awe of that hand, and so now I can talk to you from that place of sacred trust, and intuit that you are finding and guiding and connecting and supporting and lifting me even as you continue your own grand adventure.

Loving you,
Martha

Saturday 11 May 2013 — 11:38 A.M.

My darling Brian,

It was the morning of January 3rd when I woke up after a mainly sleepless night and the song "All the Way" dropped from some heavenly portal into my head—the song that pulled me back into music. Of course I was wretched and broken and quite nuts back in January, although I wasn't imagining things—it was you who gave me the idea. I'm still a mess, honey, but I've had two rehearsals with Jeff—the second one yesterday. He basically props me up beside his piano and exhorts me to open my mouth and sing. When I bawl, which is fairly often, he flips through the charts and says, "Should we try something else?"

"The Things We Did Last Summer," in particular, is hell on the tear ducts. Beautifully distracting, however, is the fact that he's taken those old Sammy Cahn songs and elevated them into the sweet surprise of discovery—each given new life, each arrangement containing none of that "same old, same old, crap" that you used to go on about. You'd be thrilled.

Jeff, my new jazz brother, is a graduate of Princeton, and an expat New Yorker, and he was just nicely back from the funeral of a dear family friend when we got together yesterday. This friend, eighty-one years old, had been a mother figure to him. She and her husband ("Your namesakes—are you related to any Jewish New York Brooks?") have always been an inspiration to him as a couple.

"All the Way," that anthem to life-long love, was one of the last songs we tackled. As an aside, it's a song that Jeff feels particularly connected to, as he once played it for an idol of his, a singer named Prudence Johnson. Anyway, I'd been worried about making it through that particular song, and sure enough, broke down crying partway through. I looked over at Jeff and realized, dear God, he was no help, as he was doing pretty much the same thing. We both broke off, laughing, and I slumped down in a chair near the piano and said, "We could do a couple more and come back to this one—I promise I'll get through it."

He said, "I can't promise the same thing."

We did go back. I tackled it with the heart and mind of a storyteller, just simply a different but honest take and he did the same thing with his piano and when it was over he wisely said, "Let's do this one just piano and voice on the 22nd."

We ate (ravenously) the supper I'd cooked and brought over and called it a day. In spite of how much of a faucet I still am, I can't wait for this concert. I've gone from not being able to hear advertising jingles without bursting into tears to a whole lot better place and I'm loving it. I love this music. Fingers crossed, however, there'll be no outright bawling, on stage, in June.

All my love,
Martha


Sunday 12 May 2013—9:40 A.M.

My darling,

Eight years ago, when we were about two weeks into our over-the-top "love affair"—not answering the phones, "sorry but we're busy," "just lock the doors, for heaven's sake," a mysterious rash appeared on your chest, and when you stood grinning at the Chinese herbalist, she shook her finger at you and pronounced, "Evil heat," and gave you something for it. It was a very hot time and we went through boxes of raspberry Popsicles.

It was the Renaissance of our lust, a time of ecstasy and growth as a couple and crazy giggling fun. I look at the sky differently now. These days without your touch, your body loving me, I pause in the middle of things and, though longing for your physical form, I'm still in love and still filled with you. You pour through my spirit like sweet warm honey.

My love,
Martha

## Monday 13 May 2013 11:15 A.M.

Brian, for many months I went around feeling Brian-less. I was Martha-and-Brian-less. Now, I am filled with you, as I was telling Kirsten yesterday, Mother's Day. Twinned with you in my spirit, I go about my days, now, feeling very Martha and Brian. Or, as our daughter pointed out, "Brian-full." So yes, I am now Martha-and-Brian-full.

My love,
Martha

# BOOK THREE


# EDEN

"Sometimes you have to play a long time
to be able to play like yourself."
—Miles Davis

Sunday 19 May 2013—10:29 A.M.

Darling,

Saturday, I moved your ashes into Rabbit the Matrix: the cardboard box inside the velvet bag with the Mr. Rabbit puppet draped jauntily over all. Then, loaded with summer supplies (Mike had already taken some ahead in his van) and, with Myra behaving not too horribly in the back seat, we headed for another season in the wooded hills overlooking the long sparkling expanse of Pelican Lake.

So here I am back at Eden. Kirsten and Mike came out a little early, on Friday evening, to divest the cabin of some of the dreck of winter's sad energies—built a fire, burned incense and sage, said some prayers to the ancestors (of which, sadly for all of us, you are now one). The past twenty-four hours have been a lovely family time and we are all now sinking into the rhythm of the place. It's still coolish, a grey day, the leaves beginning to show like little green candle flames on the branches of the trees. Water birds are just beginning to arrive, along with a few songbirds.

I'm happy and sad at the same time to be here. One of our Winnipeg neighbours, Linda Langevin, strolled across the court to see me yesterday just as I was leaving. We met halfway and she said, "You look fantastic. How are you?" then hugged me, looked at me again, all of her warm spirit in her eyes, and said, "Okay, but not okay—right?"

"That's right," I said, "and that's okay."

She hugged me again. "Have a lovely summer at your lake."

I told her I was coming back for two weeks in mid June for the Winnipeg Jazz Festival and about how much music is healing me up, but that playing around in Eden was going to be helpful in doing the same thing.

We have another gig! October 29 at the Franco-Manitoban Cultural Centre. Steve, my nutty longtime bassist, playfully emailed to say, "I'll bring pumpkins!" Jeff is arranging to have our concert recorded at the Jazz Festival. We're still waiting to hear back from Karla at the Rady Centre. ("Her audience will eat this stuff up.") Things with the music are really starting to move. Honey, now that you are free-floating, could you pull some heavenly strings and orchestrate a few more gigs? Meanwhile, I'll keep singing—being here will make my voice and my body and spirit stronger.

I love you,
Martha


P.S. 12:12 P.M.—Just talking to Alice, who said they missed me on Saturday night. We chewed the fat about this and that. Told her I'd transported your photo from the city fridge to the country fridge, and, "My God, what a handsome guy."

I told her about all the singing I was doing and how pleased you'd be about it and then we talked about how you were probably orchestrating it all—just as you did in the background in support when you were walking around on the planet.

"He wasn't just another pretty face!" Alice added.

— xo, M.


## 21 May 2013 Tuesday — 8:37 A.M.

Brian, honey—am sitting at the round white table looking out over the glistening waves of Pelican Lake. After three days of high winds and rains and dreary skies, the sun has finally come out. Scraping sounds of various aerials and leaves and the odd branch on the pale green tin roof of our tree house cottage add to the symphony of the wind now blowing across the lake from the east. I look across at the old TB sanatorium. Alice and I grew up on its grounds, daughters of a doctor and a nurse, the happy life of our family juxtaposed against the dramatic lives of the tuberculosis patients. Those memories provide, still, so much fodder for my novels.

But that is not where my head and heart are now. Right here, in this moment, I am a nineteen-year-old girl again, bobbing up and down in the water by Dad's boathouse, the canoe pulled up on shore, the sailboat moored in the reeds, and you slipping around me in the water, touching me everywhere, kissing me, hot slippery summer kisses, our laughter, the surprise of soaring birds, our youth, and my handsome freckled man with wet black curls and lake water washing over your face.

You speak to me now from every year we knew this valley together—so much to explore and remember.

This morning as I kissed your picture—you looking back at me with all your honesty and practicality—you instructed me to take off my wedding rings. "Both," you said, "yours and mine. Put them in that little dish by the bed where you always set your emerald studs at night and leave them there for a while and think about it. We're still married in spirit. Wherever your life takes you, you don't need two thick gold rings weighing you down. I love you, now take them off, honey." So I did—slid them off, dropping them heavily into the dish—and here you are, in all the lightness of your being, right behind my eyeballs as I write this, and strangely, for me, the weight of widowhood seems to have lifted, somewhat, too.

I'm loving you and you are loving me,
Martha

## 23 May 2013 Thursday—6:55 P.M.

Honey,

Our country friend Marilyn and I have been living in each other's pockets for the past several days. We drove to Killarney this morning and took Myra to the vet for a checkup. After that we dropped her off home and took Marilyn's truck to the fields and dig places looking for artifacts. I found a very large white bone, staring up at me from the black soil.

"Pick it up and take it home to Myra," Marilyn, my avocational archaeologist friend, instructed. "That's a buffalo bone and as it's near the Hokanson site" (the site named after her, because she discovered it) "it'll be about a thousand years old."

Myra was somewhat taken with it, chewed on it a bit and then left it by the door—it's probably a little stale.

More songbirds keep arriving. They start up around 5:00 in the morning.

It's so peaceful here. When you aren't settled inside my spirit, part of you goes whisking around the cottage at night, a constant flowing circle, keeping me safe and content. I will never let go of that part of you—I need to know that you haven't vanished completely. Nobody but me knows just how deep our connection was and still is. But how sad that I can no longer have you physically.

A lovely breeze is blowing up, now, from the south end of the lake. I can see you, still, in my mind's eye, standing at the deck rail, your orange fleece, the back of your head. But visit me in my dreams tonight, honey—I sure would like to talk to you.

All my love,
Martha

## Friday 24 May 2013—8:14 A.M.

Brian honey—just finishing breakfast, the dog banished to the breezeway. We took our accustomed morning jaunt up the hill after I did my yoga and she roared into the ravine, found a dead deer carcass, and after several minutes (I'd already come back to the house) she reappeared and threw up deer hide and live maggots all over the carpet. Sigh. Kirsten and Mike's cat, Oonagh, is so much easier to be around. Except, of course, for the bag of bread she found on top of the fridge yesterday, tore open and got busy in with her clever little paws. Kirsten calls them *les animaux*, and there are many hours of the day when I think of them fondly.

I'm going to spend the day thinking and singing, *sans animaux*.

We got another gig!

Thinking of you with a song in my heart, my darling.

Your darling,

Martha

## Sunday 26 May 2013 — 9:26 A.M.

Brian—Marilyn was here for a day and an overnight and a walk through the woods that at one time led to our mutual friend, Dr. Doreen Moggey, whom we always called Daisy. We so loved her, her sharp mind, her sharper tongue—a psychiatrist who could cut you down to size whenever she felt it was necessary, which was all too frequently for many: a bit of a land mine, our Daisy, especially in her dotage. In my heart of hearts, as you'll remember, I found her adorable, but of course she'd have loathed to be called that.

"She either loved ya or she hated ya," Marilyn said with a grin.

"Ah, but we were among the fortunate chosen, the loved few," I smiled back.

Daisy is gone now, sadly, but her spirit still moves all through the beautiful thirty-one-acre stretch of heritage bushland (once hers) with its steeply banked narrow trails and the lake dropping below (I think our friend was part mountain goat) that run between our property and the house she lived in for many decades. We went in search of her wild asparagus (they aren't up yet) and found, instead, a lot of wood ticks.

Back home, there were oranges split open and laid out on our deck railing for the orioles (such flashes of colour and brilliant song soaring up from blue of lake and into the sky)—and then there was food for us, wine, a movie, and many chats.

Now Marilyn's off to her own cabin and I'm here alone at our treetop Eden, singing and getting stronger all the time in my voice, doing yoga stretches, researching Sammy Cahn stories and listening, also, to the wind and the ticking of the clock and the scratch of this pen as it moves across the page.

I'm full of hope and sorrow in equal measures.

It seems the only writing I'm interested in these days (the novel's going to have to wait) are these letters to you (always in search of you) even as you watch me from your shapeless consciousness—as our favourite singer would say, "the dearly dead prevail."

I am so much healthier, physically, than I was a very few years ago when it was me that we worried about. I'm so ready to move and shape-shift in the world, and welcome and embrace those hopeful possibilities just beyond my touch and knowing. You are still the companion of my soul, and I believe in your moveable spirit—the things you place in my path are utterly surprising (you always did like to surprise me) and mysterious. And as you continue to say "Hello" in this manner, I continue to be open and open-hearted about whatever you send along.

Marilyn and I were talking this morning at breakfast about communication. "People are so disconnected in this world, girlfriend," she said. "They don't connect with their surroundings. They sit and text nonsense."

I told her that artists are the connectors, the communicators, and seem to be one of the last groups who, as a whole, do this. Art reaches out and touches people. So I guess that's my job now, honey. You've set me to this task—spreading the message in music and words about the importance of real connection. We are, after all, interconnected on this planet—with each other and all living things.

That oriole singing on the deck, just now, is a heavenly message from you. "Put down that pen, Martha, and shake the sorrow out of your heart and sing. Sing for your life and all the good things we had together and still do have—and yes, I love you."

My love,
Martha

## 29 May 2013 — 12:31 P.M.

Brian, my darling—people are talking about the orioles in this valley. There have never been so many. Flames of tropical orange fly through the air, float into the trees, bob along the deck railing, all backlit by the lake. Orange everywhere. It's the year of the orioles, another message from the portals of heaven, and their song, also, is everywhere, as you are everywhere. "Martha," you say, "keep going, keep living your life. Keep your senses, all of them, open. See and hear and smell the summer. Don't look over your shoulder to see where I am. Here I am, behind you, got my arms around you, catch you if you fall, my voice right next to your ear—trust that."

My love,
Martha

P.S. Tonight, for Marilyn and me, I'm cooking a tomato tofu dish that you cooked here at the lake last year on 18 May (recorded in my blue journal) and it was one of the last things you cooked. This dish is an honouring, darling.

My heart,
Martha

## 30 May 2013 — 1:45 P.M.

Darling, darling, darling, tomorrow would have been your seventieth birthday. How sad you never got to celebrate it—you should have grown into an old man. You would have been such a beautiful old man. We would have been beautiful together.

Sorrow.

So instead I'm sitting in the blue chair—with you not across from me as you read the paper. The day is blustery. The wind and rain are whipping from the east straight across the lake.

Tomorrow, I'll go to the city and pick up my longtime editor and soul sister, Shelley Tanaka, and bring her out here for an
overnight and hopefully she'll be able to see enough of the physical
place that she's fallen in love with in my novels. We'll have a good
time, anyway.

Missing you with every beat of my heart,
Martha


P.S. 2:55 P.M.—Well, honey, here I am a little while later. Karen just
returned my call and set up an appointment for us to get together
and talk when I get back to the city in a couple of weeks. She told
me that she's just recently officially retired from the United Church
and that that has its own grief, but it's okay. I was telling her about
Natalie Goldberg's teacher, Katagiri Roshi, who would offer up to
her the old Zen adage, "Always be a beginner." Karen responded
with her own favourite quote from Sam Keen, who said something
like, "The only question after can you begin, is, can you begin
again?"

I then told her about the orioles and she said, "Oh yes, he's sending you messages just to remind you, 'here I am!'" She chuckled.

I said, "People don't quite believe it when I tell them these
things."

"Right," she said. "They roll their eyes."

"Uh-huh."

"Well," she said, "I firmly believe in this stuff. I believe that
their energy can cross the boundaries between this world and the
next and that that continues for quite some time. And you are such
a special couple—it's a privilege to meet both you and Brian."

So there you have it, darling. All I need sometimes is a little
heads-up in confirmation that I am still, quite literally, rocked in
your love.

xox,
Martha

P.S. She told me to keep singing and keep writing these letters—from your lips, to her ears and lips, to me.

P.P.S. She also said people don't believe this stuff if they've never been there, never been through it.

## 1 June 2013—4:00 P.M.

My darling Brian,

A heartening visit with Shelley, long-time editor and friend. "You won't know what you've got until you're finished," she said, as we talked about "Letters to Brian." I wondered aloud to her, "Should I put our life out there so publicly? Is what I'm planning to do bravery or foolishness?"

"Neither. Keep on with it. Just know that anywhere you want, you can push the delete button."

I'm going to go easy on myself the next couple of days, sleep and just be in nature with your loving spirit, the orioles, the pelicans who glide like thunderclouds over the surface of the lake, and les animaux. I am at my best with you—when I am simply alone with you. Grief is tiring, nature restoring, and your love for me is endless as is mine for you.

My love, my Love,
Martha

## 3 June 2013—7:25 P.M.

So, Brian my darling, I went to see Dr. G. today—your GP in nearby Killarney for the last six months of your life, the doctor who, above every other medical person, gave you the most comfort and compassion and who saw us as a couple. Over the many times you went to be checked for blood tests and all manner of other things, she kept you safe and comfortable and provided me with the only place where I felt that your care, during that long devastating time, was one of cradling and not isolation. She'll be my GP for the next several months that I'm here in the valley.

I've run into her a couple of times since I came back, always greeting each other with open hearts and quick hugs, but today was the first time I sat down with her—she and I without you. We looked at each other for a very long time, a steady gaze that said it all.

"Ah, Mr. Brooks," she finally sighed.

She usually offers me a tissue, but in this instance reached for one first, then quickly offered one to me.

I broke down crying and said, "I can never lie to you—my medical condition is sorrow."

I added, "I want to be brave and live my life."

She suddenly covered her face with her hands. I thought, she's so young and far from her homeland. A wife and mother with two small children. Yet she manages to reach out to all her grateful patients—I'm not the only one. She's the one who's courageous.

I told her a few more things to allow her to recover. She finally raised her head. We both wiped our eyes.

"Do you want to take my blood pressure?" I offered.

She didn't at first answer, but wiped her eyes again and asked, pointedly, "How long has it been since you had your blood work done?"

All my love,
Martha


4 June 2013—5:32 P.M.

My darling Brian,

Called Jeff about the script I'd emailed him for the concert.

Then I went over to the old Heintzman and we found the

beginning note (don't know why I didn't think of this sooner) for each of the songs we're doing—making rehearsals at the lake so much more effective.

I told him about how the Heintzman was, for you, an albatross. How much you wanted to get rid of it. How nobody else did, and we'd all rush out of the room whenever the subject arose—which was frequently. You'd go on about how much space it took up, and so on.

"But now," I said, "his ashes are up there on the very same piano, and when I fretted about that, just a little bit, to my sister, she said, 'Brian would tell us: I'm no longer in a position to be offended by it.'

"However," I went on, "even if he's on top of this tinny out-of-tune piano, the CD player and the speakers are also up there and so he does get to enjoy his favourite singers."

Later, after I'd sung for a few hours, going over to the piano to find notes whenever I needed to, I heard you say, "If I have to listen to this goddamn piano all summer, I'll go crazy even if I am dead. Please get it tuned."

"What?"

"Must be someone in the area."

The ball is rolling, honey,
xox, Martha

8 June 2013—12:30 P.M.

Brian,

Myra is always eager for us to do something—stones thrown in the lake for her, walks up the hill—but she was thrilled when I stopped singing today and got out the lawn cart and knocked off the spiderwebs and came to be out here with her as the wind and sun gently bless the trees—sound of grebes below, the odd pelican bobbing along on the lake, the sound of white sails flapping in the tricky "cat's paw" winds of Pelican Lake—the weather, at last, lovely enough for sitting out.

I'm here for two more days—until my return late in June with a series of visitors, their comings and goings. It's nice to be here alone for the next bit. Alone with my thoughts before going back to the city and diving into my first public performance in a year— such a scary vulnerable thing to do—but, for all kinds of reasons, this concert is where I prove, to me, my mettle. You'd be proud. In fact, slipping as you do so easily back and forth between the thin veil of this life and the next one, I know that you are.

My love,
M.

P.S. Reading Dianne Collins's intriguing book *Do You Quantum-Think?*—recommended to me by our witchy and spiritual friend, Pat.

Collins presents a universal big picture that moves beyond "old world thinking" to ideas that exhort the reader to think outside the box. This is a book that's helping me understand my own thinking about quantum leaps: what I imagine you do, as you shift back and forth between this world and what lies beyond, and quantum thinking: what I'm trying to do in opening myself up to intuition and synchronicity and synergy and creating a space for us that, even now, allows a joining at our souls' core.

## Sunday 9 June 2013—4:21 P.M.

Darling,

I was just down at the lake throwing shale off the dock for Myra to swim after. I always gather up sets of forty stones and we were almost done our third set when I heard someone move along the dock behind me, turned, and saw it was our summer neighbour John McDonald's wife, Arlene.

"Oh Martha," she said, gathering me up in a strong embrace, her whole heart in her arms, "we were so sorry to hear about Brian."

Then she said, "I saw what a special couple you were. I know if that were me losing John—we are so close—I don't know what I'd do."

It really does take one to know one. A recognition of how deep the pain goes/must go when you, yourself, are part of "a special couple."

She made me feel less alone, honey, in a way that few people could or can. It was comforting to stand beside her and feel her affection and deep understanding. We are all connected on this planet, very little separates us, just a little flesh and bone, and yet when you meet someone who seems to look at the stars the same way you do it's such a blessing.

My love,
Martha

"THE LIFE OF THE DEAD IS PLACED ON THE MEMORIES OF THE LIVING. THE LOVE YOU GAVE IN LIFE KEEPS PEOPLE ALIVE BEYOND THEIR TIME."

— MARCUS TULLIS CICERO

## Later, 11:40 P.M.

Brian, I can't sleep. It's the last night (for a while) in Eden. Drinking some spiced tea to heat my throat. Thinking about how I believe I have a lot of life yet to live. About how, as I promised you, when I started all these letters, I would live my life with dangerous attention to my heart. As long as I have a life to live I'm going to live it.

This brings me to the surprising thought that if you hadn't got sick and died, including the year of struggling right along beside you (in sickness and in health—that wedding vow again) I wouldn't be doing any of this. I'd be settled into the comfort of us growing old together, too happy with my lot in life to even consider change. But now look at me, rejuvenating my singing career, stopping writing one book while being fired up with the idea of another and writing that book even as this pen glides across the page near the midnight hour—its very being because you died. I'm not sure what it all means in my shifting relationship with you, but I think you know that it is all unfolding just as it should.

My love,
Martha

13 June 2013—7:49 P.M.

Dearest Brian,

It has been a couple of days of reconnecting with my city. I do love Winnipeg and its people, seeing summer life on the downtown streets and in the neighbourhoods—the energy a living fabric of birds and trees and gardens and colourful clothing and colourful characters.

I went to see Karen Toole yesterday, always a necessary pleasure, as I embrace the life of my spirit even as it floats on a still pool of sorrow and do what I need to do.

Karen said, "Grief is intensely selfish and one of the most selfless things we will ever experience. When we grieve we are completely wrapped up in ourselves because we were able to love another. It's a beautiful paradox. You have to go to that place in order to heal. You're doing the work," she added, pointing at the orange journals where all these letters to you are first penned, "and what you are writing is not, as some might feel inspired to do, just a pathetic and dismal outpouring. Your letters are full of joy and hope and humour and, of course, sadness. I also really feel, through you, as if I know Brian. As if I could walk into a room of people and spot him. I would know him immediately."

We talked about Patricia Barber's "dearly dead"—what Karen calls, affectionately, "my dead." Included among those is a man who died too soon at fifty-six, Reverend Kazuo Iwaasa. He was a mentor as well as a great friend, and in a conversation with her before he died, he referred to the biblical, "Yea, though I walk through the valley of the shadow of death," and then added what had become one of his great truths: "Life is lush in the valley."

All my love,
Martha


## "INTENSIVE TRANSCENDENT RELATIONSHIP"
### —KAREN TOOLE, DESCRIBING WHAT YOU AND I HAVE


### 14 June 2013 – 11:58 A.M.

Darling,

A morning that began with more downs than ups, and then nephew Brian called from Eden about "cottage stuff" and raised my spirits. He and his brother, Todd, have of late been calling me their sister/aunt. Possibly because they're now in their early fifties and I'm still in my sixties, the roles tend to get blurred.

"I was just in the hammock reading a book and then I fell asleep, tough old life. The grass," he informed me, "is gorgeous, lush, good thing it didn't get mowed before now with that ball-buster of a lawn mower. Looks like this amazing carpet—you could roll in it, Martha."

He sighed in deep contentment and added, "I'm a happy boy. I love physical work. Don't get enough of it in Montreal. Now the gardens look great, planted a bunch of herbs and colourful annuals. Haven't found anybody with firewood for you just yet. New answering machine, one that works this time. I'm cooking gorgeous food for Todd and me. I love it all."

Another deeply contented sigh.

"Well," I said, "I'm sure Uncle Brian's keeping you company."

127

"Todd and I were just talking about Uncle Brian this morning," he said, "about how his absence and yet, still, his presence makes this place feel like home."

After I got off the phone, it rang again and this time it was Elva—our old friend whose family roots go back with us to the beginning of time. She was calling from her home in Texas but had been back, briefly, in Killarney last week visiting her mother Ruth and brother Neil, who'd told her about you.

"I'm so sorry for all you've gone through, my dear," she said. "I just had to call and reach out to you."

She told me that she had lost her partner, Alistair, eleven years ago. We've been so out of touch, honey, that I didn't even know this. And when she asked if we'd ever met him, I had to say no—although we certainly knew of him through her parents Dave and Ruth, who knew my parents and so on.

We talked for a bit, not long, before I started to cry. It seems impossible to keep back grief's tsunami, and it's always difficult with people who are fresh with the grief of you no longer being on this planet and because, like so many, Elva loved you.

I apologized, between sobs, for not having been in touch to tell her what happened.

"No, no," she said, "it is I who must do this—it's up to me."

When you and I were living back in that farmhouse in the mid-seventies with Kirsten (such a little girl, in love with rabbits, and we had, at the time, about five of them), Elva and her then husband, Paul, were on sabbatical from Urbana, Illinois. Paul was a mathematician, if you'll remember, and you enjoyed talking to him, he was an interesting guy. They were living at the time at her parents' country place, not more than a half hour from us.

During the time when you were travelling so much, trying to generate sales in the farm machine business we'd moved to the country to help grow, Paul and Elva played doting uncle and auntie to Kirsten, and I was grateful to them. Elva and I also spent a lot of time together. She is a visual artist and even did me the great service of reading and commenting on my first (quite dreadful and unpublished—thank God) novel. Later, during our final year in the "Prairie Canary," when you'd lost your work and I was struggling with new worries about what was going to happen to us, Elva wisely said to me, "Don't fret about this. Take this time and enjoy it. It may never come again."

Today, after telling me about Alistair, she confided, "I've been single eleven years. I rather like it. You never know when you might meet somebody, Martha. But if it were too soon and you married him there would go your opportunity to enjoy and explore your single life. It might not come again!"

We then talked about the dead and how they leap around, knocking themselves out sending us messages.

"Brian's full of beans," I told her. "He can't put enough 'crazy coincidences' in my path. He's been very very busy."

"Yes, busy," she said. "And you don't talk to most people about this stuff. About how it happens all the time. They just think you're crazy."

"Right," I said. "Except I'm writing a book about it."

"That's wonderful," she said, "because now you are creating a map for a previously unmapped territory."

Just before she got off the phone she added, "And there you have it."

This is not a phrase that most people use.

"Elva," I said, "not only did Brian nudge you to call me today, but just for good measure, in case we didn't catch the Universal Joke, he put his own words in your mouth. His epitaph, the saying we all attribute to the one and only Brian Brooks is, 'Shit happens—and there you have it.'"

As usual, honey, you have my attention.
xox Martha

**15 June 2013—2:45 P.M.**

Darling Brian,

Elva got me thinking—and so this letter to you is called, "The Single Life."

If someone were to ask me (which nobody has so far), "Would you ever consider getting married again?" I'd tell them, "God, no."

That's the short answer. I took off my rings, at your suggestion, not because you and I are done—which we are not—but because I have a different relationship with you now that will continue until the day I draw my last breath and slip to the other side and cleave to you again. This relationship doesn't involve "rings"—an earthly sign of someone's physical presence when they are, in actual fact, dead. I can't imagine marrying again. How could we top what we had—the very evidence of its beauty propelling me to write these letters to you. A second marriage would be second best, and why would either of us want that?

Another question: Would you ever want to live with someone?

For now, at the very least, that answer is also, "No." Whom could I live with that the living with would not flow quite badly in the shadow of what we did so well for forty-five years?

Next question: Would you consider a boyfriend?

Answer: Yes.

Question: Would you feel guilty about it? (Karen asked me the same question.)

Answer: An unequivocal "No"—you wanted that for me. But, as Karen also points out, for all kinds of reasons he'd probably have to like you, too, Brian, and that sounds like an exhausting process—especially if he'd never even met you. How would that work?

My love,
Martha

## 18 June 2013 — 11:57 A.M.

Darling — completely wired and quietly terrified about the gig and can't sleep. Going to hear Patricia Barber tonight, in concert, and it's all rather surreal. Yet here you are, close to my ear, saying, "Go and enjoy yourself, and by the way, Sammy Cahn sends his love and says, 'Break a leg on Saturday, kid.'"

xox Martha

## 20 June 2013 — 10:56 A.M.

So, darling,

I was dozing on a sofa at the Toyota dealership yesterday, waiting for Rabbit to get his oil changed, his fluids topped up, his tires checked, a bath, and so on, when the craziest thing happened. You'll remember a few letters back (May 12th) and me jogging your memory about the summer of the raspberry Popsicles, right? Mmmm raspberry. Needless to say, I haven't had one in a very long time. Sigh. Bear with me. Anyway, I woke up from my couch nap, to one girl saying, "Martha, your car is just about ready," and another Toyota girl wandering around with a box of Popsicles offering them to their customers.

"Do you have raspberry?" I asked.

"Oh, yes," she said, cheerfully proffering the box.

So I took one. By God, it tasted good. It was a very hot day— although, admittedly, not as hot as the last time I had one.

My love,
Martha

### Sunday 23 June 2013—8:29 P.M.

Well, darling,

It's taken a day to get my thoughts together about last night. Here goes:

I'll start with how, before the concert, I lurked around inside the green room, behind the invisible protective wall that I'd erected for myself. Even so, I couldn't resist checking out the window that looks onto the foyer of Cinematheque, our venue, to see who all was coming through the door. Among strangers and old fans were family and friends—many of whom spied me through the glass and waved their support. I waved back, but stayed put until Kirsten's friend Vincent saw me and came to the door. There'd be no putting him off, so I slipped out, all the while trying to look inconspicuous.

He wrapped me up in one of his big hugs as I said, "Can you keep an eye on things tonight?"

"That's why I'm here, love."

"I'm feeling a little exposed … I mean, if people rush me afterwards and all I want to do is hide …"

"Shandra and I are on it."

So damn fragile that the audience, whom I'm normally thrilled to see and can't stay away from even before a show—saying my hellos and tossing out good vibes and having to be dragged back to the green room—collectively, was a worry to me. What if I bawled, up on that stage, and filled them with either crushing pity or confusion and, either way, ruined the evening that they were here to enjoy? And what if I put more pressure than I already had on my jazz brothers as they tried to be their best, do their best—how awful that would be—especially for Jeff, what a waste of all his good work in helping to bring us to this point. Not to mention the sound guy we'd paid to record everything. So much was riding on not letting people down.

Jeff and Steve and Rob sat chatting together in the foyer as I emerged. Everybody else had gone inside. They nodded, "It's time," and stood up and we walked, *en famille*, into the venue, down through the audience and got up on the stage. There was a lot of the excitement in the room, a lot of love even before we'd played a single note.

I remembered right then and there what you'd told me once about the audience: They're on your side and want you to shine. They're waiting to be given something special. If you love them, they'll lift you up to do your best.

Ah, Brian, what a thing to remember at that moment. Were you whispering in my ear? Did you have your hand on my back? Were you and Sammy Cahn pulling a few heavenly strings?

Whatever it was, right from the beautiful melodic opening lines of "Time After Time," the concert flowed.

And here is something else: just about every jazz musician I've ever worked with, no matter how heartfelt and good they are, has led with their brains. Jeff, however—though a cerebral and daz-zling player—leads with his heart and, unlike so many, listens to the lyrics. In doing so he pulls everyone along with him. That's his good and honest gift. Steve and Rob were our in-sync band-mates—giving everything a supportive ensemble feel. As always, they had my back.

Two hours later, "Day by Day," our closing number, had the place erupting into whistles and cheers. Then it was over. I went around hugging the brothers, who were pleased by how it had all gone. I came off stage and left them to pack up their gear.

Now I was lifted up by the happy faces of the people who'd hung around to say hello. I hauled off my shoes as I came towards them because one of my toes had suddenly spasmed into a ham-merlock. Shandra suddenly appeared, such a beautiful glowing girl with the gift of joy.

"What a great show!" she bubbled.

"Oh God, my foot," I told her, laughing but in pain, hobbling along, reaching out to hug people.

"Stop right now," she said, laughing at me, pulling me down into one of the seats from where she massaged the hell out of my foot. I kept trying to hold court with everybody. Now I hated to see them go, especially as I'd missed the chance to greet them when they'd all arrived.

Later, our sister-in-law, Daryl, remarked about the concert, "It was a watershed moment for you," and your sister, Maureen, who flew in from Kelowna, said, "I was sitting in the audience with Daryl and I turned and told her, 'What a gutsy thing for Martha to do.'"

A day later, feeling vulnerable after listening to the recording of the concert, I called Jeff and said, "The last half of the show works, the first half not so much."

He countered with, "The whole thing works. It gave me chills. How long has it been since you sang in public—a year? From now on it's going to be a triumph every time you get up on that stage."

A few days before, in rehearsal, I couldn't get through, as usual, "The Things We Did Last Summer." Cry, cry, cry, and it had been like that since we started this process, back in January. Every Sammy Cahn song is so poignant. As Our Maureen remarked, "Sammy is inside every song he ever wrote." Yes, his spirit resides there. And for me, now, you also reside there, now that I've had a chance to simmer down and think about it.

I guess I have to say, hearing the concert played back, I also hear a new voice—from a heart that's been transformed and washed clean by tears. As Charlie Parker once said, "Music is your own experience, your thoughts, your wisdom. If you don't live it, it won't come out your horn." My voice sounds different from earlier recordings because of this new texture and backstory and edge, none of it there before you got sick and lived out a year with brain cancer and then were taken from us.

We have enough good recorded material for at least a demo or, it's entirely possible, a full CD. Who would have thought that out of so much sorrow could come such heart-sweeping joy? Your second wish for me—that I continue with the music—has, most profoundly, come true.

All my love,
Martha

28 June 2013 9:15 P.M.

Darling,

I'm back here at the lake with Our Maureen. We have been reminiscing about you—you, everywhere in this beloved place, in its many spaces that your hands touched over and over again through the years—the fixing, the building and cobbling things together. The "art installation" high on the wall over the kitchen sink where, one summer, you hung (with your gift for amusement and beauty) Dad's eighty-year-old canoe seat, layered with years of paint, its patina of age, streaks of robin's egg blue and olive brown, creating an image of reflected lake and sky. Everyone, seeing it for the first time, pauses, and with a kind of bemused admiration, inquires, "And what's that?" And the two oils by Paul Mari, hidden for years inside dark garish frames, given new life when you remounted them by turning them backwards in their frames, the exposed backsides rustic and charming, enhancing the images— one a rather Spanish-looking interpretation of the old TB sanatorium across the lake, where I grew up.

The old shed, outside, nestled against the woods, that you re-panelled in brick-red tin and then, on the wooden bracing across the doors, you painted a slash of Kodak yellow. The cedar deck that you built thirty years ago makes standing in the cottage and looking out at the lake from the floor-to-ceiling wall of windows seem like being in a tree house. The grey lichened boards are a testament to your integrity: cedar should never be painted, the old boards only replaced as needed. The red kitchen floor, the red painted counter sides with their splash along the floorboards of, again, that beautiful orangey yellow. The small cabinet between fridge and stove that you fashioned with cast-off wood and a Japanese handsaw. All of this, by the way, suggesting more creativity and heart than a bucket of money—another reason why I love you. I could go on—the plain, handsome library shelves by the fireplace that you built with Dad, and near the front entrance to the cottage the French lilacs that you planted, low growing, clipped each year, their hypnotic perfume attracting yellow butterflies that swoop in like enchanted spirits.

Every inch of this place has been touched by you, every inch a memory of you, every inch of me a memory of you. And so I'm here, once again, with the long stretch of summer and early fall before me, creating word and music patterns in the space you nurtured along for us all, season after season—your legacy a touchstone of who we are and where we have been and where we are going. You got it just right, honey.

My deepest love,
Martha


## 29 June 2013—2:45 P.M.

Brian—took a drive with Our Maureen today down some of the country roads that you and I trekked along on hot summer days and cool fall days over the past several seasons here at Eden. Most notable (the car crunching gravel, trailing memories like happy ghosts) were the old rail bed road and, after that, the road that you fondly referred to as "The Ponderosa" for its alternately California/ Old West movie look—hills, with lone spreading trees, the long grassy slopes absolutely female in their undulating curves. The sky-and-cloud backdrop at their tops begs a horse or two—riderless or otherwise—to suddenly appear over the ridge. You often said you'd like to go in there on horseback.

On one of your birthdays, I toyed with the idea of renting a horse and getting permission from the landowner for you to go beyond the fenceline that skirts the road. You could have gone riding in what looks to be acres and acres of unbroken land. But I never did that, and now, in my mind's eye, you ride a spirit horse in there—free to come and go as you please because nobody bothers ghosts!

I also remember the day you and I were walking along the tree-lined sun-dappled Rail Bed Road—Drummer, happily chasing rabbits and shadows up ahead—when you looked up beyond the trees to a sky-backed grassy hill with its line of cattle fencing and came up with titles for Annie Proulx–type Wyoming stories. One you would call "Fencing," another you'd call "Waxing the Hearse," and a third you'd call "The Piano Tuner."

You never did try your hand at fiction writing, but you were always dreaming up stuff, including ideas for films. So when you told me, half-jokingly, that I could use your titles for something of my own, I said, "No way. They're yours. There's a kind of brilliant haiku/short story going on in all of them. Write them down for me—I want to see them, on the page, in your handwriting." So you did. Above it all you wrote: "Brian's short story collection started today with the titles of the first three."

I look at it now, set down in my blue journal in your rounded, half printed/half written script that is an almost perfect mirror of my own.

Slightly dyslexic, and few people knew this, you struggled with spelling but never reading. You were a man who, in your later years, read mostly non-fiction. However, when I was nineteen, you introduced me to Tolstoy and Chekhov and Ibsen, and, just for good measure, J.D. Salinger. You were a visual person with an eye for architecture. My, what a mind you had. What a thinker you were. And what an eye you had for the world.

My love,
Martha

## Wednesday 3 July 2013 — 8:00 A.M.

Brian —

This letter to you should probably be entitled "Dogs We Have Loved." Let's start with our "Problem Child," the lanky eighty-pound labradoodle Myra, our current dog. Born on Hallowe'en in a puppy mill and rescued by an animal shelter called D'Arcy's A.R.C. with about seventy-five other dogs (same mill) at around three to four weeks of age. Neurotic from the start. Afraid of stray garbage bags. An hysterical barking shrieking banshee in the car—lurching (from a secured seat-belted position in the back seat) at all oncoming trucks and semi-trailers. Hasn't found cow-pie or rotten carcass or any other disgustingly odiferous thing that isn't either rolled in or eaten or both. In other words: you can't take her nowhere.

She came into our lives just after my second "brush" with breast cancer, followed by two years of relative calm and then, pow, your diagnosis, the ensuing craziness, and then the holding pattern coloured by uncertainty and stress. I'm afraid, honey, that she's gotten short shrift.

And so, this winter, with new family housemates, including the adorable grandcat, Oonagh, there has been some dog training. No more leaping up on people the instant they come in the door. "The Golden Paw" unleashed by Oonagh when proper distances are not kept. A "sit, wait," "look at me," and "take it," before being allowed to eat. All of this has led to a calmer dog and therefore a more pleasant dog.

The last time Myra was in the car, when we drove out from Winnipeg with Auntie Maureen, she was not too bad. I would tell her, "Don't bark at that truck," and she would watch it go by (my eyes quickly flashing to the driver's mirror) with no hysterics. This command was repeated about fifty times over the course of our two-hour-and-fifteen-minute trip, with the same, "I've got this covered, we are not being attacked," tone.

On Canada Day she was proudly carrying around her new favourite "stick"—a three-foot-long, eight-inch-thick pole, denuded of bark that I picked up for her early this spring near a beaver lodge at the Souris River. If you'll remember, we've all loved firing things off the deck for the dogs to fetch, and Maureen was getting a kick out of doing the "kyber toss" for Myra, who would go leaping in and then thrash violently through the undergrowth looking for it. Anywhere between one and three minutes she'd reappear, log cantilevered between her teeth, face full of cobwebs and leaves and dead bugs.

But this one time, the log landing on top of the bushes and staying there instead of crashing to the ground, she couldn't find it. She came back up on the deck, but after some encouragement from Maureen, headed back down again. She finally spied it and half-stretched, half-climbed partway up a neighbouring oak, all the better to appraise the situation. Coming back down she then did the most amazing thing. She got her front paws on the bushes where her log was trapped and started to push, rocking back and forth, stopped, looked up at the log, and went back at it again.

Maureen fretted about how that with all that thick bush, and the lake dropping a hundred and thirty feet below, the log might not be reclaimed.

I remembered you saying, "Dogs need a challenge. This one's bright. Let her figure it out for herself," so I told your sister, "If she's successful, you'll have done her a favour. She's bored most of the time."

Just as I said this, didn't the log come flipping out of the branches, landing with a satisfying woody musical thud on the ground. Myra, not wanting to leave anything to chance, grabbed the end and dragged it backwards, bum swaying, up the hill and out of the bush. She was in high good spirits. Perhaps, like her mother's singing in concert, it was a watershed moment—witnessed by two excited laughing women who were lavish in their praise.

Another installment about our other dogs later. Myra is enough for now. This is her moment.

My dearest love,
Martha


6 July 2013 — 3:19 P.M.

Honey,

It's been a couple of weeks of visitors, first your sister, who was closely followed by Alice and Eddie.

I went to Moore's in Killarney with Eddie and we purchased some cedar panelling to reconstruct the inside breezeway wall where carpenter ants have been residing until very recently and, as well, much lateral rain seeped in from the east and caused quite a bit of damage.

I remember loving going to Moore's with you. That brilliant "off-cut" you purchased from them a few years ago for fifteen dollars and then used to fashion a serviceable counter for what has become our much used laundry centre.

Eddie was ecstatic about the cedar—wonderful-looking material, and much less expensive than the same thing he'd looked at in the city and would have had to (somehow) haul out here.

He said to me, "Of course that'll be offset by having them deliver to Ninette."

"They deliver free of charge," I informed him.

Moore's told us, "Might be a few days before we get there, though."

That was yesterday. The Moore's truck arrived this morning, along with an envelope with ten dollars and change tucked inside and a deep apology that they'd overcharged for materials.

Eddie stood around looking slightly stunned as the young driver was getting back in his truck.

"Not only do you deliver, but you give me my money back," Eddie called out to him. "What the hell kind of an outfit is that?"

Driver smiled and called back, "One that I hope doesn't go bankrupt and put me out of work."

"Moore's is doing all right," Eddie said later. "Look at all the construction that's going on in this valley—it's all Moore's. A bit of good will goes a long way."

He was still going on about them as he and Alice were leaving. I think we're going to be spending a lot of time there this summer, honey.

Wish you were here to enjoy all of this work and effort. We all miss you.

Cry, cry, cry, my man. Nobody like you.

All my heart,
Martha


7 July 2013—9:02 A.M.

Good morning, my darling,

Got up, did yoga, sang "All the Way," cried, sat down on the bed, cried. Myra came rushing in to see what the fuss was about, consoled me by sitting on my foot and angling her neck and head over my knee. Then I made us pancakes—not as good as Mike's Sunday Morning Special, lacking as they did chocolate almond milk and spelt flour and his *je ne sais quoi* touch, but they were pretty good, anyway.

Later, a little stroll with Myra among the birds and green smells and blue sunny sky and mosquitoes and honeybees all liberally mixed with those spirits of transformation—orange butterflies. Butterflies everywhere these days. Alice and Eddie brought me an early birthday present, a gorgeously researched and photographed and written book called *Manitoba Butterflies—A Field*

*Guide*. At 245 pages, the writer, Simone Hébert Allard, has done her homework.

I write this in the chair where you always sat, the sun sliding across the pages of my journal, the wind and birds creating an inside/outside song line through the screens, through these spaces of Eden. I am wearing our rings, today—also an occasional thing—and I feel close to you.

I am alone today and will have several more days, alone. I am discovering who I am, alone. Smarter than I thought. By necessity, one sharp brain—except on those occasions (and they are now occasions, no longer the norm) when friends and family pitch in with the attitude that two or more brains are better than one.

And another thing, "Six months, six years, you'll never get over him," somebody said truthfully to me a while back. I suppose I won't, but six months, six years, I can't stay static.

I have also had the great good fortune of being adored by the men in my life, starting with my father and continued for years and years by you, honey. And so I take, also as my due, adoration from male colleagues, male friends, surrogate sons and nephews and brothers-in-law. When, infrequently, I am not adored, I find it confusing. In other words, yes, I'm lucky, and all of this gives me the impetus to keep on keeping on and keeps me writing these letters to you.

You are my lover, serving overseas.

You are my long-distance lover.

You are my lover beyond the veil who delivers messages when I open my heart wide enough to receive them.

All of this is making me the woman that I am becoming: smart and sad and vital and open to the open road of life.

And I love you with all of my heart.
And much more than I can possibly find the words to say,
Martha

## 10 July 2013—10:09 A.M.

Darling,

Dragonflies—airborne acrobats—cruise for breakfast against a backdrop of misty Pelican Lake. The sun breaks through here on the western slopes of the valley, but directly across, to the east, the long lines of sky and land and water resemble a Christopher Pratt painting in varying shades of grey. You would appreciate the day's gentle diversity.

I have a small piece of time in which to gather my thoughts before the next wave of visitors. Alone, preparing my breakfast as I do leg stretches on the kitchen counter, stopping briefly to stride seven steps over to the piano, find a note, return to swing my leg back up on the counter, do another ballet stretch, sing the opening verse of "Time After Time," then a vocal run reaching A below high C (not bad) and a pause, in silence, to listen to the orioles and towhees and the finches, before letting my mind ramble over this writing I've been doing and what I want to convey to you from the flow of my pen. In other words, I am in connection with the Muse of Art and these days that would be you, honey.

When I was a beautiful young girl, living on the Christopher Pratt side of the valley in that big red-roofed house with its wrap-around verandah, I would rest, on summer days just like this one, on my bed on the sleeping porch just beyond the gauzy white curtains and the double French doors of my bedroom. In this inarguably romantic setting I would close my eyes and imagine, as young girls do, just who might become the most significant man in my life. This was years before I met you, so the picture that would come to my mind's eye was always misty and grey and slightly formless—not nearly so intriguing as a Pratt painting, but then I hadn't lived long enough to understand the endless possibilities that life holds for us all—both to the good and to the bad—not to mention the many charms and challenges of the colour grey.

And yet I am still much like that young girl. I'm blessed with youthful energy housed inside a youthful spirit, good genes (when I was forty people thought I was twenty-five and thus it has continued to this very day) and yes, as well, some pretty good luck—there it is, again. As long as I stay healthy the possibilities still seem endless—granted, there is less time now than there once was—but how different this new attitude is from the one I shrank inside, back in cold December. I know you are listening (ah, yes, the dead do have ears), because you still affect every decision I make even as you keep urging me further away from death and into the light of life.

My love, my Love,
Martha


13 July 2013 – 9:13 A.M.

Darling,

Grazing over every inch of the physical life we had together, I came one day upon a piece of paper lying face up on your desk where I'd been working for several months. It had just been waiting for me to discover—written in your hand, the details on a book you'd wanted to purchase and read. So, when I was back in the city last month, I purchased the book for myself and now, on a sunny windy morning two days before my sixty-ninth birthday, I'm sitting out on the deck with Myra, reading *The Philosopher and the Wolf* and searching for you. And here you are: within the first twenty or so pages I've come across two names that frequented our early conversations on rearing our Airedale, Drummer. Vicky Hearne, philosopher, animal trainer, writer, poet, who penned *Adam's Task* and whose horse, Drummer Girl, provided us with the perfect name for a dog whose rhythmic running was more horselike than doglike—and other inspiring insights. And then, Bill Koehler, whose dog-training methods (as Brenin the wolf's lifelong companion, the philosopher Mark Rowlands, accurately points out)

144

were alternately sound and "psychopathic." I really need to reread Koehler for what you and I kept and what we rejected.

This morning's letter to you could be about me—just substitute the name Brian for Brenin. The jist of what Rowlands is saying is that what he learned about being human he learned from a wolf. All and all I could relate. These days, without you, I sometimes find myself a lesser human when I am in human company—more brittle, less self-contained. The most self-evident aspect of me alone is that our lives—like those of Rowlands and his companion wolf, Brenin—once intertwined, are no longer visible to those who knew us. Your physical absence from my side, the defining aspect of us as a couple, powerfully and painfully fills the spaces of conversation and, at times, disturbs normal human flow.

Was my previous letter to you, about how well I'm doing, in actual fact a kind of fiction? It was true in the moment I wrote it. And I know it will be true again. But here is another truth: it is on these pages, really only here, that the evidence of you is not quite gone—not to me, at least. In the privacy of this writing I can touch your face again. Sadly, to everyone else you really are gone.

So yes, I'm befuddled and bemused, my beloved, and not altogether myself, these days, in human company. But out here on the deck with Myra-dog, who is chewing a stick as I read a book you would have loved—Myra, who understands on the deepest level the complexity of your absence/presence—I am almost whole. And Myra understands ghosts. She's lived with one, the ghost of Drummer, all her life. Drummer, howling songs in the Zodiac as we blasted along on summer days over golden water. Drummer on the deck with an orange plastic ball in her mouth, flinging it onto the newspaper you were reading, then standing back, eyes gleaming, until with a low chuckle you fired it back at her. She'd catch it perfectly in her mouth, then dash in and toss it into your lap again. This time you'd lift the ball, calculate how far it would go and fire it off the deck. She'd tear after it and re-emerge not long after, up the steep hill through the bushes, and toss the ball, slobbery and poison ivy–ridden, back into the centre of your newspaper, as you said, "You can never tire this dog out." Drummer, swimming or running, bounding through stinging, pelting snow or three-foot-high waves. Drummer, who would run flat out as we snowshoed or walked or climbed up hills or traversed long stretches of dusty summer roads. Drummer, who finally, at precisely ten o'clock every night, would attempt to herd us off to bed. If we weren't quite ready, she'd stand looking at us briefly, then sigh in disgust and leave with a look that clearly said, "All right, if you guys won't come to your senses, then don't blame me if you're tired in the morning."

So, okay, honey, I get the message. I need to get up out of this chair, don't I, and give Myra some of our all-too-absent attention. Now, where the heck is that orange ball?

xox
M.


## Sunday, 14 July 2013 – 9:00 A.M.

Brian darling,

It's quite cool this morning, so I've made a fire (who says fires should only be built in the evening) and am now sitting beside it, coffee mug within easy reach, pen in hand, writing you this message from Planet Earth. This is the same firewood that nephews Brian and Todd stocked in for us last summer—long-burning, good-smelling ash.

The last night you and I spent together here at Eden, October 24, 2012, was spent cuddling—me under your long arm, enfolded by your long-fingered hands—as we watched a bright steady fire all evening, feeding it a log every half hour or so. I would have liked to have kept going just like that with you beside me, the primal snap-crackle beauty of the fire, the summer in review slowing as the peace of the place descended.

"It didn't go crazy—just kept on," you said, as we turned in.

Yesterday, I went over to Killarney to treat myself to a massage with my friend Coral, who kneaded my sore sad body into a state of grace as she said, "You'll always remember the way he made you feel." Wise Coral. Kind Coral.

Amen, my darling,
Martha


P.S. 2:40 P.M.
Went down to Ninette to pick up Saturday's paper, which was being held for me at The Grocery Box. Came back, opened it to Lindor Reynolds's column and its headline, "I'll Miss You While I'm Off Fighting Monsters." In late June, a week after her 55th birthday, she was diagnosed with brain cancer. She begins her column by saying, "Sometimes Life is a capricious old whore." Brian, I whine without you as I try to find paths of healing—in this moment. And I am not quite brave—in this moment.

My love, my Love,
Martha


## Monday, 15 July 2013—8:08 A.M.

Darling,

The letter is entitled, "Daughters and Sons—Blood and Surrogate." Today is my birthday and my present is arriving from Selkirk this afternoon for a five-day visit in the form of our "Other Daughter" Kate. Katie, who calls me "Ma" and you "Paw." Who buoyed up both her "sister" Kirsten and me during the terrible days of your illness and death. Kate, whose genesis as our daughter began when she was seventeen and coming to our home as a writing mentorship student. I have a full twenty-three years of memories with this our other daughter—whose birth parents are Scottish, Irish, Doukhobor and Lakota. She and Kirsten are both writers and spiritual people.

They find power in walking the same healing path. They confer on "medical issues." They do magical things together and apart. They are both astounded by stars and eagles and trees and thunder. They are both electric and loving women—one year apart in age.

Kirsten called from the city yesterday. I had called to sing "Happy Birthday Dear Michael Alexander Franklin Grabowieski" (who shares Kate's Lakota roots and whose birthday, also, is the day before mine) into the answering machine. She was calling back to wish me an early Happy Birthday and to ask, "Are you excited about Kate's visit?" All this amidst sounds of vegetable juice being processed (kale and lemon) and perogies being warmed gently in the pan for the birthday boy. She also offered, with some prodding from me, that she has recently begun the hard work of grieving for you. That's the way she operates, honey—choosing her time, the right time.

"I'm lucky to have Mike and Vincent," she added.

Before I left Winnipeg in June we drove out of the city to purchase organic herbs for Kirsten's garden. In the back seat was Vincent, his arm around his current girlfriend, as he explained to her, "Martha taught me everything you need to know about schmoozing with Icelandic women."

He loves the Icelandic roots that I passed down to Kirsten, and so I humoured him by firing a Viking glance into the back seat.

"And what's that?" I inquired.

"You have to agree with them," he shot back. "And if you are in conversation with three of them at the same time—remember that time at Pat and Gary's Christmas party, in the kitchen—?"

"Vaguely," I said, because it would have happened about fifteen years ago.

"Anyway, the most important part," he went on, "is that you have to make all three of them feel that each of them is right. Even if you don't have a clue what it's about. Because Icelandic women will run circles around you until you are stun-fucked, if you get my meaning, and so agreement is the healthier choice."

Vincent came to my gig with a migraine he didn't bother to tell me about. In other words, like Mike, he is another surrogate son who (I am a blessed woman) adores me.

All my love,
Martha

Tuesday 16 July 2013 — 10:37 A.M.

Darling,

Another cool morning—rain, logs crackling in the fireplace. Kate and I are having a transforming one-on-one time. She has been unwell and finds, as do so many others, that this is a healing place. She has also, by being here—loving you as she loves me—given me back a piece of myself, a piece I didn't know had been missing all this time.

As we stood yesterday on the hill at the windswept park that is dedicated to Mom and Dad and all the good TB work they did on a pittance—both what they were paid and the budget they were given to work with—I felt, somehow, my childhood with them and my adulthood with you merge. Sorrow was replaced by wild hope. A heaviness lifted from me, flew off over the valley and dissipated in the clouds, as all the little moments that you and I shared while taking our many walks in this valley, holding hands and minding the day, the comfort of just being together came flooding back. Even as I had been trying to write about it, what I'd tried to recapture on these pages seemed to be a dream, but standing with Kate, solidly with Kate, as with her painterly writer's eye she marvelled at the memories this valley holds with all of its shimmering ghosts, you came back to me again. Today, I am content.

I love you,
Martha

Sunday 21 July 2013 — 9:36 A.M.

Darling,

Kate and I spent six days together in which, we both agreed, time was kind and stretched and gave us each a thousand little moments of healing. Kirsten called us on Friday evening. We both dived for the phone and one of the first things Kate told her was, "Ma is coming gloriously into her own."

The walks! Kate gave me the courage to take all three walks that you and I used to take, her youth and enthusiasm giving wings to my every step. We picked wildflowers and she took dozens of pictures, which included a photo session with me, one morning, because someone had requested a photo for a jazz promo, and as my most current promotional photo was taken in 2001, it really was about time.

The dog training! Myra worships Kate's every command: Queen Kate. Goddess of Dogs, Kate. Kate of Treats and Praise. And yes, honey, as we've known all along, Myra is very smart. Armed with Kate's training skills, maybe we're starting a new chapter together.

And the meals—salads and chicken and Kate's new favourite, risotto. All eaten with a stunning view of the lake; one meal taken as a wild storm swept down the length of it and crackled with drama and filled us with awe. During the six days of our retreat we cried and laughed and filled the lonely corners of each other's lives with new places in which to softly land and create.

However, Saturday afternoon, after she left, I came back to earth by attending an outdoor funeral in which one of the mourners asked how my winter had been and when I told him you had died he expressed (brief) sympathy, looked down my top and then said, "We should go out for lunch sometime."

Later, when I was talking to Alice on the phone, Eddie piped up, "If he goes out with Martha…."

"No worries," I said to my sister, "I'll kill myself first."

P.S. later, 5:00

So okay, honey, I put your ring back on, third finger left hand—I'm hoping that will dissuade the riffraff. Then again, it might just inflame them. Sweet Jesus. Other than that this day has been terrific. I gathered a small bouquet of wildflowers as I walked along Dry Weather Road this afternoon—bergamot and sage, what a healing fragrance. It was spitting rain. I heard thunder and saw lightning in the distant darkening sky and soon turned and started back home—but all in all it was an exhilarating walk.

xox Martha

## 25 July 2013—8:10 A.M.

Dearest Brian,

I went into town to check my emails yesterday, sitting in Rabbit outside The Hot and Frosty, Ninette's Internet cafe. Driving back, I turned to you, to your spirit in the passenger's seat and said, "I feel really good about this writing I'm doing, darling."

I heard a chuckle. Felt your hand slip along my shoulders and then to the back of my neck to give me a warm squeeze—such a typical gesture—before you said, "What did I tell you."

As I cull through these letters to you, adding here, deleting there, brightening all but not tampering with the order in which so many synchronous events have taken place, or with the spirit in which they've been written, I am constantly surprised by the fact that a story is evolving. The writer, that artist part of me, observes you being brought into the light—and after all my years of writing and reading it still seems miraculous that words can do that—but now, of course, I'm also at the centre of my own evolving story. To me as a fiction writer that feels a little strange, but really it shouldn't. Writing a novel, for me at least, is organic; I never know how things will go until I get there. So here we are as this story happens, as my life unfolds with you, and without you, as we take a journey such as my characters would take—except, of course, I'm real and you're real. As you would say, "That intrigues me—what's next?"

My dearest love,
Martha


## Saturday, 27 July 2013 – 8:24 A.M.

Dearest Brian,

I count off the months since you died, now eight. Pen in hand, just back from a morning perambulation around the yard with Myra, I sit at the round white table, looking out at the lake, reaching every so often to touch the screen saver on my iBook so as to make a photo of you and me reappear—one that I've been loving to look at lately. The photo was taken three summers ago by our friend Jeffrey Canton. There we are, smiling, me tucked just so under your arm, head resting against your shoulder. We're both in green, me in an emerald hooded sweater, you in a dark forest fleece, your red cap pulled jauntily over your eyebrows. We stand against the backdrop of a fat summer hill outside the fenceline at the Ponderosa walk.

The blue ink from this pen flows—a Zebra, Sarasa .07. The pen—now a talisman—has been refreshed several times with refills since I began these letters to you in December. I think it belongs to Jeffrey, appearing as it did on our dining room table after his last visit, a devastating time for him, as it was just a week before you went into the hospital for the last time.

So now, after bringing two Maureens into this unfolding story of you and me, we move from jazz brother Jeff to book brother Jeffrey—and this one has been such a deep part of our lives for the past dozen or so years. He's coming from Toronto to the lake in early August, his usual time to visit before he goes back to teaching classes at York University in September. It will be a happier visit than the last one.

Larger-Than-Life Jeffrey, this big hirsute man—Kirsten's self-proclaimed Fairy Godmother, inveigler of all things bratty, who for her first marriage, on her wedding day at Eden (terrible marriage but what a fabulous magical party) came dressed as the Fairy Godmother of the Bride in a wonderful African getup that involved sandals and beads. He and I both wore corsages. It was a Midsummer's Night theme wedding and people really got into it.

Soul brother Jeffrey—whose subject heading in the email he sent to me when he first found out about your diagnosis, was "Sweetheart!" I love him. He loves me. And he so loved you. I can hardly wait for his visit. He has a big shoulder to cry on and a cavernous spirit to fall into. We'll drink dark ale and I'll cook him yummy things and we'll talk our heads off about everything. Bright, bright man, is Jeffrey: children's book specialist, professor, book reviewer, book lover, loves my books—which was how we first met, even before you knew him; Jeffrey, who will always pester me to write yet another book, even if I whine. You've managed to cover your bases, honey.

My love, my Love,
Martha


Monday, 29 July 2013 — 8:44 A.M.

Darling,

Another cool morning. Myra and I went out just as it began to rain—me dressed in your yellow rain slicker. I escaped inside you, peeking out at the weather, surrounded by this garment I always loved on you. I went to the woodpile, where I loaded my arms with logs and sniffed the crisp air, and the dog went tearing around the yard with a bright green ball in her mouth. All dog joy, she then whipped past me and did her crazed circus poodle loop twice around the shed as I stood back and laughed, the logs growing heavier in my arms. After that, I staggered back inside the cottage and she followed me and watched in gleaming-eyed celebration as I dumped long-burning ash and oak into the firebox.

So many ghosts followed our happy trail this morning—you among them. You, standing in the warm light inside the workshop. You, pulling garden shovels and rakes from the shed. You, calling to Drummer before coming back inside the cottage, dripping rain, chuckling, pulling off the yellow jacket, strolling into the kitchen to kiss me—your skin cool and damp and healthy from the weather.

The summer, here at Eden, is flying by, half behind me, another half still to be lived. On Wednesday, Alice and Eddie and nephew Todd arrive for a working visit—five days of reconfiguring the breezeway wall with good-smelling cedar panelling. Todd, a lovely gentle soul, informs me, through his mother, that I will also be shown how to bead caulking around the bathtub, a useful skill. Right after they leave, Jeffrey will arrive. As much as I love my sister, I am looking forward to the company of men—gentle men.

All my love,
M.

Tuesday 30 July 2013 — 8:26 P.M.

Darling,

If you'll recall, the number eleven—and variations of the number one—featured in our lives a year or so before you were diagnosed. We'd both look at the clock at the same time (in the kitchen, in the car driving to the dog park) and it would be 11:11 or 1:11. We'd shrug and laugh—it seemed such a bizarre coincidence, even if it meant nothing. Your definitive diagnosis came at 11:11 on the 11th day of the 11th month of 2011. Ever after that, the 11th day of the month leading up to your death bore a special significance as in, "Well, we've survived another month." I still mark that day in my heart on the 11th day of every month since you left us.

If you'll also recall, somewhere back in April I mentioned that I'd applied for an arts grant with the Manitoba Arts Council—threw my hat into the ring with about forty pages of these letters to you. I've been lucky with these grants before, but that doesn't mean that it is ever a done deal. I must say that I really hoped it would successfully come through. But the day that I thought I might hear, positively, came and went. I kept going down to the Hot and Frosty to check my emails, sometimes quite hopeful, other times not. These letters to you are so very personal—was I just fooling myself that anyone would want to endorse them, much less a jury of my peers? I began checking my emails twice a day.

This morning I checked. Nothing. Such a sinking feeling. If I didn't get the grant, a validation that I was actually onto something (even if I continued writing these letters to you) would I have the heart to continue trying to make it all into a book?

I put my iBook away and started the car, glancing at the clock: 11:11.

"Just hang on a minute," I heard you say. "You don't know that you didn't get it. You just think you didn't. Don't start second-guessing things just yet."

I went home and a short while later phoned My Maureen.

"Call them," she said. "Just call and ask when they're letting people know."

"That sounds like a good idea," I said.

"So if it's a good idea, then will you do it?"

"Yes."

"Phone me back when you know."

The receptionist at the Arts Council said, "It's been ten weeks. You should be emailed this week whether or not you're successful."

Maureen said, "So you'll know this week. At least you'll know."

Darling, I waited until 3:30. Then I went back down to the Hot and Frosty, opened my computer and waited for the emails to come in—five. Two emails had been sent not even an hour after the first time I checked, both from the Manitoba Arts Council. And I knew—I got the grant for *Letters to Brian*.

I'll just let you weigh in: "What did I tell you?"

All my love,
Martha

31 July 2013—12:20 P.M.

Darling Brian,

Last night I was in such a good mood that I scribbled on a piece of paper: "I see my life in lush tones." This morning that thought was pretty much answered as I drove down the steep road that accesses Eden. Joseph Haydn's Cello Concerto No. 1 came over the airwaves on CBC. Sunlight fell sumptuously on the road and the shimmering surface of the lake beyond. Just as I turned into our driveway, a hundred or so dragonflies flew up in front of me, their wings dancing with life and music. Nature means for us to remember days like this, honey. So, perhaps, did Joseph Haydn. And so, I'm certain, do you.

All my love,
Martha

Monday, 5 August 2013—8:34 A.M.

Honey,

Our seventy-eight-year-old brother-in-law, Eddie, and our fifty-year-old nephew, Todd, hammered and sawed their way through the weekend, pausing to drink endless draughts of hot strong coffee, the occasional beer, do lots of head-scratching and bantering and make trips back and forth to cut boards in the work-shop, followed by Myra, who forgot pretty much all of my dog training the minute she realized she had new playmates.

The east-facing breezeway wall was the cottage project that you most stressed about getting underway and you would have happily tackled it last summer if you'd been well. Throughout this weekend the all-important vapour barriers and plywood boards came together in a nice tight fit around the casement windows that look out through the trees onto Pelican Lake. The light in there is beautiful, and as we are a family of artists (the weekend builders, respectively, a photographer and a lighting director), the aesthetics were celebrated.

The cedar panelling—"Finicky to put up, but fun," says Eddie—will be done on successive four- to five-day trips to the cottage. He is already dreaming about refurbishing the casement windows retrieved forty years ago by Dad from the old infirmary at the san-atorium. "The windows must be at least a hundred years old," said Eddie. "Got to show them some respect."

So now the plan is to also re-putty the panes, ten panes to each window—four windows on the east side of the breezeway and three windows on the west side. "And then I'm going to paint the wood around them red—hopefully the same shade of red that Brian used on the rest of the place. Except I'm already having trouble finding it because he used up all the paint he had and didn't leave any cans lying around."

Ten minutes later: As I wrote that last sentence I remembered that, with your usual attention to detail, you'd tucked away some paint sample strips. I recalled seeing them in an odd place, and then I remembered: they were in the dresser drawer in our bed-room where you kept notes and folders on various projects. There, under four operating manuals about the Zodiac and its motor, were the paint strips. I phoned Eddie in Winnipeg and said, "I found six possible shades of red—all from Benjamin Moore."

"That's the best paint there is," he responded. "Hang onto those strips."

At one point during the weekend, he and Todd came in from the shed. I couldn't see them from where I was in the main body of the cottage, but as they laughed and talked I swear that for a moment I thought you were with them. Then I realized that your voice and your laugh was coming from Todd—a quick landing of your spirit that caught my ear and made my heart stop.

Maybe you were also with them as they went out on the driveway again to play a lively game of what they called Phantom Ball with Myra. Sometimes when people are teasing a dog they'll throw a pretend ball and the dog, especially a smart dog, is not fooled for more than about six seconds. But this was different. This was a game that Myra got into because there was such playful goofiness but it was serious play. She'd sit in front of Eddie and Todd, waiting. One of them would make a hand like it was holding a ball and show it to her. She'd watch intently as an arm drew back and then the phantom ball was hurled purposefully down the driveway or across the yard. She'd run after it, retrieve it, tear back and drop it at their feet. I stood watching part of this performance from the bedroom window. Everyone was laughing, including Myra—with that tongue-lolling Ha Ha pant that happy dogs make. Later, Eddie said, "That dog is so smart she's spooky. She actually got to the point where she'd gauge how far the ball would go before she'd fetch it."

Apparently she played quite a few rounds of Phantom Ball before she got tired of it, looked at them as if to say, "Okay, that's enough," and after that she ran off, found a real stick, came back, dropped it at their feet, and then stood back, waiting.

My love,
Martha

Thursday, 15 August 2013 — 11:14 A.M.

Darling,

It's been ten days since I've written—a pretty long stretch to go without checking in. Jeffrey came on the sixth, and he left yesterday. Now that I'm alone with you again, I have much to tell.

I'll carry with me forever an image of you and Jeffrey at the Winnipeg Symphony jazz gig, back in 2003 (he'd flown in for the concert)—me coming off the stage, you and him getting up from your seats in unison, and in greeting, like a couple of brothers, all smiles. Jeffrey—also an inveterate jazz fanatic—and you were twinned, back then, in the mutual joy of promoting this music passion with me at the centre—phoning back and forth at the time of the release of *Change of Heart,* and he was instrumental in getting us that three-day gig at Toronto's Top O' the Senator—the place was jumping; such great players, David Braid, piano, Mark McLean, drums. A twelve-year history with you and me and Jeffrey, in which he's always also been a promoter and supporter of my books.

As he and I talked and took walks on Dry Weather Road and the Rail Bed Road and the Ponderosa Trail, and ate sumptuously and read and relaxed and missed you, I also realized that Jeffery embodies for me a special kind of home, one that you of necessity vacated, yet still watch over. Echoes of your care and support ripple through this bright sweet man.

While he was here he had a dream about you, what he called "a visitation," in which you appeared in your "normal Brian way" and simply said to him, "Everybody."

"Yes," I said to Jeffrey, "he does visit everybody. And he's still taking care of us all."

My love, my love,
Martha

## Saturday 17 August 2013 — 8:45 A.M.

Brian honey,

I'd give my two arms to have you back again. But here's the thing: I'm happy. Happy as ever a woman could be without the love of her life. Does that make sense? Yet, even as I write the word "happy," I understand that I am always treading water in a still pool of sorrow, and that no matter how blue the sky, or how exquisite the clouds above me, farther down is a whirlpool. What lies beneath is what I examine, daily—resilient though I am—and there is a date coming up this month that I must look at before it gets here, August 26.

Even though I realize that wedding anniversaries loom large in many people's minds, our own day would frequently have been forgotten by us but for the kind remembrances of friends and family as they phoned or trotted us out for dinner or dropped cards in the mailbox. If you'll recall, we spent a nice chunk of the day of our fortieth in the sack. At Marilyn's insistence we drove down to her cabin later, flushed and happy (I have no idea what I wore—certainly there wasn't a corsage involved) and she and her brother Ronnie made us a vegetarian supper, eaten outside as the waves lapped against the shore.

Sometime during that weekend, we took a walk down the Rail Bed Road and you picked up a rusty iron ring left over from the old railway tracks and stood, chuckling, looking down at me, placing the "ring" on my finger and asking me to marry you. Then, before we walked on, we tucked it down by the side of the road, thinking it would be there every time we walked past—even if we didn't remember the exact spot. Over many many walks in ensuing summers we did look for it and of course it never showed up again. I was telling Kate about "the ring" as she and I walked that same stretch, in July.

Katie, a romantic, said, "Here you go, Ma."

She simply reached down and found one—for sure not the

exact one, because this one was smaller—and she dropped it into my open palm.

I've kept this one, put it inside a little bag with a small flat stone and some sage and cedar and bergamot and a few other private treasures, and stuck it inside my pillowcase. The stone often jingles against it, making a bell-like musical note. I went to the piano to find it, and to my surprise it's "B" below middle "C"—reminding me that your initials BB, for Brian Brooks, will not, for as long as I am alive, be far from my tender ear.

All my love,
Martha


## Monday 19 August 2013—10:13 A.M.

Dearest Brian Brooks,

Kirsten and Mike were out for the weekend, their first since the beginning of the season. Kirsten and I went picking juniper. I made them saskatoon pie from the stash of wild berries that Marilyn and I picked a couple of weeks ago. Mike got up on the roof and checked out the rain gutters—"plugged full"—and did a beautiful job of mowing the lawn. There were naps and chats and jokes and a playful "family portrait" that Kirsten snapped of the three of us from where we lay on the deck, our heads clustered together like the petals of a weird flower, all hair and upside down smiles and giggles. "No squinting, 'kay?" Kirsten said, as we tried to shield our eyes from the sun and look into the camera and fend off the dog.

I've missed them—they've generously deferred to a longer than usual stream of summer visitors—but we're going to try to make it up with more weekends out here later in the season. First they're taking a much needed holiday to Banff. We had an early birthday for Kirsten. She said she was glad to have it early—knew that last year when they were out here on her actual day that it would be the last birthday she'd celebrate with you. "This makes it easier," she said. "I've kind of been dreading it."

I signed her card from us both: "Mom and Papa in spirit." She liked that. That first card without you signing it would have been too sad. Without you around to hug her and say, "My favourite daughter," to which she'd always giggle and say, "Your only daughter, Dad"—your shared forty-year joke.

All my love,
Martha


## Tuesday 20 August 2013—8:20 A.M.

Dearest Brian,

The letter to you is entitled: Don't-Go-Down-There Road.

Last night, after supper at Marilyn's, a beautiful chilled beet soup and johnnycake, which we both remarked you would have loved, we got into her truck and drove over some back-country roads that I haven't been on for a while. She wanted to suss out this year's crops of high-bush cranberries and bittersweet vines and I was happy to go along for the ride.

It was a sweltering evening and we bumped over the ruts in her air-conditioned truck past ripening fields of canola and wheat and soybeans and then squeezed down narrow trails, scraping past overhanging hazelnut bushes and splashing through deep mud puddles made by all the rains we've had this season.

Marilyn chirped away like a happy bird, singing her joy about this and that including, as we drove past, the Kruger Site, and her sweet dreams of finding more treasures there—six-thousand-year-old arrowheads and scrapers and points and stone hammers and bits of clay pots.

I regaled her with memories of you and me (a little further back on the route, and about four years ago) as we harvested a thick crop of highbush cranberries—you, all six-foot-six of you, in your sky-blue shirt and blue nylon pants and Crocs (your beloved Crocs) as you reached higher than anybody I ever knew to pull berries into a yellow pail.

Anyway, as we lurched along the trail the "puddles" grew larger and I noted in my head that there was, really, not much room to turn around and it would be a very long way to back out.

At the end of June, Our Maureen and I went down the Rail Bed Road, more accurately a trail. We drove in the back way and got into a place where the gravel was deeper and more slide-y than I remembered, and the trail was barely wide enough for Rabbit to turn around. There were sparkling sloughs on either side, and the water had seeped into the trail and stood glistening just below the surface of the stones. It was a very long way to back out, but I would have done so if I hadn't somehow managed to turn us around and then slowly charm us out of there. Once out we con-gratulated ourselves, and I told Maureen, "Brian would *never* have driven down this part of the road. I could hear him warning me not to and I should have listened."

"Why didn't you *say* something to me, girlfriend," Marilyn muttered when I told her this story just after we sank up to her axles in "goose-shit muck"—sloughs on either side. No amount of rocking the truck or coaxing it was going to get us out of there.

It was a long, hot walk back to the main highway. She hadn't brought her cell phone. I, of course, don't own one—but even if I did, it would have been where my bag was, at Ninette, in her house.

Just off the highway is the McKay farm. As we panted and sweated our way towards it, I tried to distract Marilyn with another story of my own pure blind luck.

At the time you and I were living on the farm at Ninga. It was a deeply cold Saturday morning in January, about 35 below—where Fahrenheit and Celsius do a meet-and-greet. There were sun dogs on either side of the sun that day. The snow was deep but the roads were passable. You and Kirsten had stayed home while I ran errands, a perfectly normal thing to do in most any weather in the country. Returning, I stopped at a farm to pick up some face cream from a lady who sold cosmetics and then took one of the many back roads home. This one hadn't been ploughed but it did, at first, look okay, although I knew that once I'd turned onto it I couldn't change my mind—and of course you know why: the VW Rabbit I was driving, my hands-down favourite car before Rabbit, had a standard stick shift whose gears consistently iced up in freezing temperatures. I'd learned to compensate, that was all part of the adventure, but at this point in my errand running two gears had iced—first and reverse. What an exhilarating time I had when I discovered, going down into a gully, that there was more snow there than I had previously gauged! As I'd lost reverse, there was no other way to go but straight on. I gunned it through the gully. I flew through a swirl of snow up to the top and kept on going like Evel Knievel. However, tantalizingly close to the turnoff, the car got hung up on a great pile of snow and that was it.

I turned off the motor and stepped out into bone-numbing cold. Not more than a hundred or so yards away was a farmhouse. I walked briskly across the road, up their short driveway, knocked on the door and there was no one home. Nobody in the country locked their doors in those days. So I went inside, was greeted by a black cat who was thrilled to see me, took off my boots, wrote my hosts a thank you note and phoned you.

"Call the guy whose farm you just left," you said, "and ask him to come and pull you out—he'll be well equipped to do that. And then drive back to town as fast as you safely can and pull inside the shop at the Esso station and let those gears thaw out. Call me when you get there."

I turned and said to Marilyn, "And it all worked out."

Marilyn, who in all the heat was alarmingly red in the face, looked grimly ahead and said, "People lock their doors now, girlfriend—I hope somebody's home at the McKays."

She was—Lisa McKay of the many beautiful cats, cats who sauntered up to us, lay like small tigers in the grass beside us, watched in regal repose as Lisa brought us chairs in the shade, tall glasses of ice water, her cell phone.

Marilyn sat fanning herself, used Lisa's phone to make a few calls and, after that, with much gratitude from us, our hostess drove us back to Ninette.

Marilyn waved and smiled graciously, watching her drive off as she said to me, "I left my house keys back in the truck."

She lives on a street of relatives. Her nephew Rick is three houses down. He and his wife, Julie, were home and paused to cheerfully chide Marilyn and give us more water and do some head scratching, and then we all got into their enormous high-off-the-ground monster truck and lumbered back to Don't-Go-Down-There Road.

Her son Karl called her later in the evening and said, "You two women are trouble, Mother—we can't turn our backs for a minute."

I called her today to find out how she was and she told me, "We won't go down that road again. But there are *other* roads. We'll go down those."

All my love,
Martha

## Thursday 22 August 2013 — 8:45 A.M.

Dearest Brian,

Yesterday, I was talking on the phone to our friend witchy Pat. She is one of the few people who has known us since we were all very young. Back in January, when I handed her a pen, she wrote a letter to you in which she said, "Dear Brian, I know that your favourite colour is orange (and that you are, even in your ecto-plasm!). It is the colour of creativity. But in our leadership work, Gary and I will call it the colour of constructive disruption. You will say and do things and then sit back to see what happens. A social experiment. Carry on, dear friend. Walk this new path. I know you will do it well. Martha is walking a new path now and with the solid foundation of all that you are together. It makes her strong and forever loving. Love and hugs, Pat."

Pat is always ready with heart-full pieces of advice to carry me across the river of sorrow. An amazing friend.

Last night there was a full moon, a blue moon, which is a relative rarity, and the second full moon of this month. Anyway, she told me that the August moon is also called, by some, The Corn Moon—in which thanks are given for summer's harvest and prayers offered up for courage in the coming year. She then suggested that it might make me feel good to honour the occasion.

Several years ago, when I wrote the book *Two Moons in August*, I had Sidonie, my young protagonist, lamenting the loss of her mother and describing that second moon as a big full cheater moon—one where everything was changed and would never be the same again.

For me everything is changed, too. Last August the table on the deck was always set with a cloth and a pot of wind-riffled wildflowers, and, with virtually no bugs to bother us, we took our evening meals at that table, our chairs side by side.

This year the table has stood unwashed and cobwebby, abandoned to mosquitoes and the elements. However, last night, for whatever reason, the bugs seemed to have died down, and so I did as Pat suggested and had a ceremonial tea of sorts for you and me as blue twilight fell over the lake. First I washed the table, set it in its rightful place near the grey railings at the edge of the deck, and placed on it a fresh cloth and a pot of wildness—bergamot, sage, juniper, purple blazing star, goldenrod and prairie grasses, a white candle, and some of summer's harvest—a red-skinned potato, an ear of corn, a small ripened tomato and a dish of blueberries. Next, I carried out two chairs and set them side by side looking out over Pelican Lake. I made two cups of tea, spiced tea in a flowered mug for me and your accustomed green tea (with a thirty-second steeping!) in the red mug you always liked. Then, side by side, you in spirit and me in the flesh, we sat and watched an immense pink moon rise over the eastern slopes across the lake. I left it all, later, bathed in moonlight, and went to bed.

I am grateful for luck and for gentle nights such as that and for a rich harvest of memories and, most of all, for the strength and courage I continue to find in you.

All my love,
Martha


## 27 August 2013 – 8:37 A.M.

Brian darling,

It's the day after what would have been our forty-sixth wedding anniversary, and now I start another year without you. I'm sad today as I sit and write this letter and try to pull you back to me in memory and in spirit.

Alice and Eddie were here for a few days and the cedar wall in the breezeway is really coming along. Only a couple more panels to put in place. Eddie's now talking about hickory mouldings. "The stuff I was going to use isn't quite right," he said.

You would love all this effort. A cottage such as this is not a house, not a full-detail residence, but a place full of memory and handsome corners—a place to dream and look out at the lake in all its moods and seasons.

"It *does* look like a Christopher Pratt painting," Alice remarked yesterday morning, looking out, as she slowly wiped dry dishes by the sink.

Yes, here we have cobbled together artistry observed from lives that are lived well.

However, here I am, missing you as I drag my pen across the page—in the middle of the page in the middle of writing what looks like a book—and I falter, honey. And so, once again, I go in search of you hoping that that will help. I go through my old notebooks, looking for a moment, anything, and up pops 12 April 2011:

"Went down to the kitchen where Brian was doing up the breakfast dishes, wiping dry a red cup. I told him that every time I read over Isabel Smith's TB memoir, *Wish I Might*, I learn more about the nature of her disease, always finding useful details to authenticate my own fictional heroine. I said I go through periods where I worry whether I can pull off my own book and then I stop worrying and go back into the manuscript and settle down. 'Years from now,' I said, 'I'll look back and say I should have enjoyed the process of this novel more.' 'Yes,' Brian said, 'and you'll say, now that's the way to write a book.'"

Thank you, darling—a message from you that gets me out of the doldrums and reawakens me to your voice and support and guidance. You were a self-contained man—as assured as the simple drying of a red cup, placing it shining on a cupboard shelf, setting down the towel, turning to place your hands on my shoulders, the morning sunlight, warm and purely there as it glanced through our kitchen window.

All my love,
Martha

## Wednesday 28 August 2013 — 8:44 A.M.

Darling Brian—

The leaves are just beginning to turn. As I sit at the table and write this letter to you, beyond the window a single dried oak leaf dangles from a branch on a spider thread out of reach of its greener brothers. It spins and flutters in a breath of wind.

And yet we are in the middle of a heat wave, everything becalmed. Even the most eager sailors have, for the time being at least, abandoned their sailboats to various moorings, and, as it is a weekday morning at the end of the summer season, they are all likely back slugging it out at city jobs while I remain here, contented enough.

Ah there, I just lifted my eyes from this paper and the spinning leaf seems to have fallen to the deck—such is the passing beauty of this passing season, another one without you—and maybe that's why these past few days I've felt so wistful. Frankly, I'm in the dumps, honey. Glad to be here. But not glad to be here without you. Attached to you like that fluttering leaf on a spider's thread. And now, as I look up, I find it again! By God, the eyes do play tricks—the leaf's so thin and it had come to a stop, sideways, so as to seem to disappear. But it hasn't gone and is holding on. Spider's thread is apparently very strong and by its very nature clings, like memory, like you fluttering and disappearing until I find you again.

"I'm right here," you say. "You just have to look a little harder these days."

My love, my Love,
Martha


## 29 August 2013—9:04 A.M.

So darling, yesterday I went down to the bottom—fought going there and finally gave up and just hit it. Called Alice around 5:00 P.M. for an emotional band-aid, which she gladly gave. Then by late evening, feeling more settled, I started listening to the rough cuts of Jeff's and my possible CD.

The phone rang and it was Kirsten.

"I thought you were on your way to Banff," I said, coming to.

"I'm sick," she snuffled, "and Mike's loading the car."

"Oh, honey, I'm so sorry you're sick. What a terrible way to start a vacation."

"Some of my customers loaded me up with healing teas," she went on.

"Have you been taking oil of oregano?"

"Yes. How are you, Mama?"

"I just miss him, that's all, but I'll be okay."

"It's okay not to be okay."

"I know," I said, thinking that that applied to us both.

It's weird to always be the one who is comforted. If I ask how she's doing, she'll turn it around and ask me the same question. If we're both in the same room and I say, "Just fine," she'll squint at me like a one-eyed pirate who only trusts the roiling sea until I fess up.

I sent her off to the upstairs linen closet to find the sewing kit, which was one of the reasons she'd called, and said I'd water the plants when I came into the city on Friday.

"Help yourself to the basil," she said.

"Will you be okay driving this late?"

"Mike'll drive. I can sleep."

"I'm glad you called. You're going to have a wonderful time. I'm excited for you."

"I know. We're excited, too. Call Mike's cell if you need us."

"I'm absolutely fine."

"I know that," she said.

"It's just that it felt like Dad went AWOL, somewhere—like he was really gone."

"Well, he's been busy. He's got a lot to do these days."

"Yes, but here's the thing," I said, wiping away tears, smiling, "let me leave you with this good image. I took a drive down Dry Weather Road this afternoon and I said to myself, 'If the blue gentians are out that'll be a sign from him.' They've shown no sign of life this year—I went last week and there was nothing and I left feeling disappointed. But today I went, and the ditch where I usually find them was practically lit up with cobalt blue."

Kirsten laughed.

"And Kate's been saying how he's not exactly subtle in trying to get our attention," I went on, "as in, 'If I present you with a burning bush, then will you get the picture?'"

Kirsten laughed again and said, "They must get so frustrated with us mortals. We can be so dense."

There aren't many people I can have that kind of a conversation with, honey. Anyway, by the time we got off the phone I actually think she was feeling better.

We've taken such different directions with our grief. She skirts the edge of it, it seems, and watches me fall in. She's taken it as her job to do so. But I keep waiting for her to take her own turn at falling in. It's way past time that she did.

All my love,
Martha


## Saturday 31 August 2013 – 9:37 A.M.

Darling—

Somewhere between getting up at 5:30 yesterday morning and driving to Winnipeg in a dense fog that pretty much covered the southwestern part of the province, and roaring around in the city, and getting back here at 7:00 in the evening, I had a revelation and it's this: I'm no longer nuts with sorrow. Over the past summer months I've managed to get my head on straight. This doesn't mean that I'm past it, out of it. Widowhood is a boot camp and just when you think you've done the work, grief plays another sly hand. And yet, honey, this life I'm living without you—your death that we didn't account for—is, in what remains of this decade, pretty darn okay. Especially when I remain open to possibility—that Emily Dickinson quote, "I dwell in possibility." Possibility opens up a music life beyond what my jazz brother and I are currently working on. Possibility keeps me thinking about the books I've yet to write. Yesterday during a meeting with Jeff he commented that some of the strongest works of artists are made in the home stretch of their lives, echoing the same thing you often told me. Of course my whole mood is also lifted by the fact that we've decided to go ahead with the CD, him producing it—things are really coming together.

All my love,
M.

## Sunday 1 September 2013—9:11 A.M.

Darling—

Kirsten called yesterday from a campground in Banff, sicker than when she left—unexpectedly and dramatically so. They'd almost gotten into an accident with a woman who careened past them in her car and summarily crashed into a dumpster and Kirsten had gotten out to console her. All in all Kirsten was not a happy camper, too sick to move much from their tent, suddenly overwhelmed with missing you and in tears. I said to give it twenty-four hours, that the worst of the sickness was likely behind her, and to just settle into the beauty of where she was. We agreed that she'd rather be in Banff than anywhere else at the moment (all those fragrant pines) and that you were with her.

"His hand, gently squeezing the back of your neck as he would do," I said.

"Yes," she sniffed.

"Three times means I love you, right? I love you, my favourite daughter."

We talked for quite a while. I reminded her of all the wonderful trips you and I had taken in that tent and all the good energy that it held and still holds.

"I feel better," she said, after a lovely silence fell between us. And I knew that she was, at least a little bit.

Mike had rushed off to get her ginger ale and packets of green tea and broth and he got back just as we were finishing our conversation and she handed him the phone.

"She thinks she's ruined everything for you," I said. "The trip.

She told me. And she said that you told her she was a crazy girl, that she hadn't. And of course she hasn't."

"We aren't taking a trip," Mike said, cheerfully. "We just decided to get in the car and come to Banff. It doesn't matter. We come. We go. We stay. Whatever. It's all good. The tent, by the way, is brilliant," he added.

"I know," I said happily, "a regular Gypsy caravan."

"We're calling it the Tent Mahal—it's luxury camping, for sure."

All my love,
Martha


## Midnight, same day

Darling,

So many memories of the days when you packed everything into the Hyundai ("It's full. Time to go," you'd say, as I'd desperately try to hand you something else). We'd then load Drummer into the back seat and off we'd go on a grand adventure, across the country, pitching the bright yellow Tent Mahal in off-season campgrounds, snuggling warmly in thick sleeping bags that we zipped together, sleeping soundly in the scented darkness.

A vestibule near our feet provided room for Drummy to curl up. Sometimes she shifted around and the little brass bell we'd hung from the "ceiling" would tinkle and remind us of all the travellers in all the countries of the world who have traversed the land to the sound of tinkling bells.

So many great memories of unusual campsites. One, you'll remember, in a remote corner of Saskatchewan's Grasslands National Park, not a soul around, our campsite overlooking a moonlike landscape with prayer circles of ancient stone. The next morning you stretched in the shimmering light and put your arm around me and drew me to you and I listened to your heart as you told me about the dream you'd had—or was it a dream—in which a deer came by and stuck her head inside the doorway of the tent and watched us sleeping. I told you about my own dream of a young Dakota warrior with a red strip painted down the centre of his scalp, who sat wrapped in a blanket all night just outside in the sage-smelling grasses. We agreed that we'd been cradled by magic while we slept.

Another night in a deserted campground in northern Saskatchewan, we took the cover off the top of the tent so we could see the stars through the screens, and we were treated to the green shifting northern lights as they danced like ghosts above us.

Another night, another summer, we packed everything into the Zodiac, boated about seven miles down the lake, pulled into the hilly shoreline and made camp overlooking the lake as the moon came up. Next morning, as I got out of the tent, a fox ran past with a rabbit dangling from her mouth. She tore up the grassy hill from the glade where we were so beautifully perched and disappeared without Drummer noticing. Later, as we packed up to leave, Drummy was torn between two treasures that she had discovered—a large beaver pole and the time-bleached femur of a cow. She worried over them, pacing back and forth, trying to choose. We finally threw the pole in the boat. But she insisted on the other one, too—so we let her take them both home. Over the next few years we got such a kick out of watching her carry that immense leg bone around, and so did guests who ask, "What the heck has she got there?"

When Drummer died and we buried her near the cottage, you put a large ochre-coloured rock over her grave and then left the bone as a marker beside it. A year later Myra was thrilled to discover it, prancing back and forth with it in her mouth. We laughed and just let her take it over. I found it the other day, half gnawed, and propped it back up on Drummy's stone. We'll see how long that lasts. Anyway, life goes on around the old place. And so does death in its inevitable cycle.

I love you,
M.

2 September 2013 — 9:36 A.M.

Darling Brian,

I'm sitting out on the deck with the chickadees busily fluttering overhead and the sun blasting beautifully on my hands and pen and journal. It was a cool night. Went down to about ten degrees and not much warmer in the cottage. But the weather report says we'll have another warm day today and everything is absolutely glistening and golden.

A couple of sandhill cranes just flew overhead in a very blue sky, making their distinctive rattling cries. The birds seem to be on the move these days. Many of the songbirds have left and now the eyes and ears are drawn to these other migrants. This summer two golden eagles nested somewhere nearby and lately a larger one and a smaller one (evidently this year's crop) showed up to show off their acrobatics. A cedar waxwing has just landed to feed in the chokecherry bushes beyond the deck, all bright rusty colours, with his face mask like a bandit. I recall three summers ago when lime green worms were hanging from the oaks and a band of thirty waxwings moved into the yard for about ten days. One morning they simply up and left, and the worms were gone, too!

Yesterday, Myra and I left the cabin and took a stroll through the heritage land. The foliage of summer has finally died down, making the trails easier to follow, as long as you are sure-footed. Walking through the bush, once Daisy's, carrying a small lightweight broom, I thought of her, well-respected psychiatrist and well-known eccentric.

"It'll be my turn soon to be 'the crazy lady,'" I thought.

One day, in her later years, I saw her walking up her road with its overhanging bushes and trees, her beloved and unpredictable dog, Brandy, panting at her side. Wearing her usual gloriously mismatched outfit, she carried aloft a large feather duster. I was in the car and we waved merrily as I drove past. Our Daisy/Doreen, the soul of down-to-earth practicality, was demonstrating that a feather duster—or, failing that, a small broom—is a perfectly useful item to take on a walk at summer's end when an abundant crop of spiders spin webs ceaselessly. If you are walking anywhere they've been, which is everywhere there is bush, unseen sticky strands in your face and hair can quickly turn a pleasant stroll unpleasant.

Call me crazy, but cobweb-less.

I love you,
Martha

## Tuesday 3 September 2013—10:37 A.M.

My darling Brian,

I spent the day reading and came across a piece about Edward Livingston Trudeau who was a visionary in the tuberculosis movement and the founder of the Trudeau Sanatorium. In a presidential address before the Congress of American Physicians and Surgeons in 1910 he said that "optimism may, and often does, point to a road that is hard to travel, or to one that leads nowhere; but pessimism points to no road at all."

The TB sanatorium, where my sister and I grew up—where Dad was a surgeon and Mom a nurse—was modelled in spiritual and curative and physical beauty along similar lines of the first viable TB sanatorium on the continent—Trudeau, nestled in the Adirondacks, in upstate New York.

And it was at the Manitoba Sanatorium, at Ninette, where Alice and I were beautifully brainwashed into a life which at its core honours the brand of optimism that Dr. Trudeau purported.

I remember you saying, Brian, a few weeks after we started dating, "I used to wonder about the San at Ninette. I'd hear song requests going out on the radio to patients there and yet it sounded like kind of a bleak place. Then I met you, somebody from there, and you're the most upbeat and gorgeous girl."

This was a couple of months before we got in your little red

Triumph, just before Christmas, and drove out there, and you fell in love with the place—"My God, it's as beautiful as you said it was. Who would have thought such a place existed in the middle of the Manitoba prairies?"—and with my family, especially Dad, who immediately took you under his wing and gave you his fond affection, fatherless boy that you were, just as I hoped he would.

I have such a tender memory of you and Dad in 1988, the last summer of his life. After twenty-five years of being father and son, a longer time than you had known your own father, you sat at the table together—looking across the lake at the sanatorium—and you took his hands, those hands that had performed so many life-giving surgeries, and gently manicured his nails. I watched the two of you, two of the most profoundly influencing and loved men of my life, and thought about how such a simple act can bring such depth to a moment. It's the glue in all those tough and heart-full and brave ways we find in going on. This is probably why, right from my own difficult illnesses as a kid through, in later life, my breast cancer and your brain cancer, plus the other usual and unusual trials that life always hurls at people, I've kept the optimism that our parents nurtured in us.

And it's optimism that fosters the kind of gallows humour that Kirsten and I appreciate and share: "Dad always said things could be worse. Of course, he had brain cancer at the time he said that."

It's one of our ongoing jokes. Levity also helps in the journey through optimism.

And optimists are given such a bad rap in the world. If you are an optimist, you are somehow suspect of being unrealistic. But, come to think of it, all these letters to you are a testament to Trudeau's contention that optimism is the harder road, while "pessimism leads to no road at all."

And so I rest my case, honey.

Your loving and sometimes travel-weary wife,
Martha

## 4 September 2013 — 8:54 A.M.

Darling,

Dear God, we have bats in the house. Not one bat, but two—they often travel in pairs. This makes their removal to the great outdoors a challenging responsibility. They cannot be killed or injured in any way.

If you'll remember, we've both loved the bats, but even with your extraordinary height you never once offered to deal with them—you wanted me to. As for most people, when they flew around inside the house they creeped you out.

Anyway, if somebody's been careless (and these days that would be me) and forgotten to close the fireplace flue before going to bed, they fly down the chimney after a fire dies and come in that way. Two or three times a season, if you'll recall, I rescue these little creatures—named, appropriately enough, Little Brown Bats. Wings outspread, tip to tip, they are the size of sparrows. Their bodies, however, are the size of moles. And, as you know, I've always been very good at their catch and release. Todd and I handled one this summer, him holding a big extension ladder and me, armed with a turquoise dish towel, climbing to the rafters in the main room of the cottage. Our nephews have expressed to me that around bats they turn into hysterical eleven-year-old girls—these fifty-plus-year-old men—and so it's up to their sister/aunt to go bravely forth.

Anyway, the two that are currently in the cottage are not so easy to deal with. They have been flying around, terror-stricken, all morning and will only land briefly before taking off again like bats out of hell. They are exhausted and so am I.

## 10:00 A.M.

I finally managed to corner the bigger of the two. I wasn't about to tackle the extension ladder by myself, but was able to use the shorter ladder when he landed at the top of the wall near the bathroom and hung by his toes, desperately trying to recover. I swept him up in what has become the bat towel, and he screamed his head off as I took him outside and released him to the wilds of Eden. His mate (I watched her do this and it was so adorable) crept tippy-toe behind some books, folding her wings in behind her. Horrible person that I am, I whipped the books off the shelves and, thus uncovered, she took off for the vaulted ceiling, where she is now hanging in a miserable attempt at camouflage.

Dear God, another sleepless night. Myra doesn't mind the bats. Excitable as she normally is, she regards them as birdies, blinks sleepily at them as if it's perfectly normal to have birdies, or bats, firing around the bedroom at midnight.

I'm going to go now and take some of Marilyn's brother Ronnie's fragrant sweet little crabapples from the freezer. In the months to come I'll use them, as I am doing today, to fill buttery delicate pie crusts. This gentler activity will take my mind off the bats.

I love you,
Martha


## 5 September 2013

Rescue accomplished at 9:00 this morning. Didn't hear a peep out of her, she was so sleepy as I gathered her up and took her outside and watched her graceful flight into the morning sky. By now she's probably joined her mate. What a lovely lucky thing for her.

Amen, my darling,
xo M.

## 7 September 2013—10:00 A.M.

Dearest Brian,

Am sitting outside with the animals, enjoying a glistening day in this fleeting month that sits on the cusp of two seasons.

Further to my thoughts on the topic of optimism. In 2007, when I clinically died and then came back, I was aware that I really should not have lived, that the fact of my being back in the world was altogether amazing. I was treated during my thirteen-day stay in hospital as an oddity, and also with tenderness—medical staff kept checking on me, pinching themselves, shaking their heads, going away again. You and Kirsten and our sister-in-law Daryl would hold me in your gazes—afraid that I'd disappear. I'd been on an epic journey and so I know bore the marks.

And I had had my own "near death" experience, not so unusual—almost everyone I know, knows a friend of a friend— and by all given accounts every experience exudes some kind of peaceful understanding of what death is. I was no different. I came back from being cradled in that sacred hand intuiting that there really was nothing to fear, that something bigger awaited and that the sacred dwells not only without but also within.

But you, my dear, observer of my drama and long-time student of your own spiritual path and your own unique (and with you, it could only have been unique) manner of experiencing an altered consciousness, were well on your way to intuiting that there is something beyond the veil. Death always intrigued you. You believed that the soul did not depart the body immediately— that it hovered around for a while. When your beloved Aunt Ada died several years ago, you told us all, "We're not going to rush her out of here." And so we didn't call the funeral home for several hours, not until we'd all had a proper chance to say our goodbyes. You read to her from *The Tibetan Book of the Dead*. Kirsten read to her from *Paddington Bear*. And so on. You instructed us well.

When you died, after two weeks in hospital that ended in three days of laboured breathing, we missed the actual moment when your heart stopped beating. Exhausted, we'd gone home to sleep. They called just before we were getting ready to leave the house in the morning to say that it was "a matter of hours"—but it wasn't, we arrived at your bedside ten minutes after it happened. Thing is, honey, you were still there. Your spirit shimmered at the surface, along every long beautiful inch of you. You looked so peaceful, but also so there. We all sensed it. And you stayed with us for three hours as we sang to you and told stories and the staff at the hospital left us alone, and Lloyd, your roommate, sat guard outside the door just in case anyone forgot. It was a proper send-off. I know it pleased you. It pleased us. But goodbyes, leave-takings, do so wound the heart. Cry, cry, cry, my man. And yet I'm left with that merciful feeling that you didn't just simply vanish, you went somewhere.

Karen Toole was so right in saying you are a joyful spirit now. I hear you in the wind and in the cry of the cranes as they fly overhead and in the waves as they lap against the shore. You are above me and below me and inside me—your being, now, so much vaster than the physical.

And that, my sweet, is optimism writ large.

I love you,
Martha


Sunday, 8 September 2013 — 9:36 A.M.

My darling Brian,

If these letters to you tell a story of how one moves past grief to acceptance, as I think in part they do, then I guess I have to say I'm not there yet. I still search for you. Examine, daily, this amputation that makes me not quite whole. The mask of "getting on with things" is one I put on and then take off again. I'm never more than a memory away from wanting you to come smiling through the door, reaching out and gathering me into your arms. I miss your arms—that's the naked painful truth. Tears spring up at any old time, from standing in grocery queues to driving past an abandoned grey farmhouse that you always said you'd like to photograph and never did. The old structure is still there, on my way to Killarney, and as I drive through that memory flocks of crows scatter from a sagging rooftop into a cloudless sky.

So I go on and make music and write books, working through it all, not so graceful in my own spirit as you are in yours, my challenge not to give up surrounded by the essence of a man I'll always long for.

In one of the notebooks on the process of writing my novel, I wrote, on March 11 of this year, "The question I always have to keep asking myself is, what is my heroine's journey? How is she changed at the end of it all? I suppose coming to any conclusion will also involve the question: How do we live with uncertainty? So how did you do it, darling?—when your thought processes were so compromised. And yet you did do it. We did it together. You had me—I was your gift, cheering you on, keeping you on track, just as you had done for me so many times before. You said to me this past summer, 'We do for each other. We take turns doing that.'" Indeed.

Are you taking care of me now? Without question. Do I know how it will all end—where I'll be at the first anniversary of your death? Haven't a clue. And that's honest. Honesty—something you deeply valued.

I love you,
Martha


P.S. Later.
Just talked to my cousin Agnes, who just turned ninety-two—always a vastly cheering experience. She told me she'd had a dream about her dearly departed Hugh. "I was at a funeral," she said, "and

I was flipping through the Order of Service trying to find the words to a hymn that we were all standing up to sing. And then there was Hughie beside me. I didn't so much see him as I sensed him there. And he was strong and young like he used to be. I leaned my head on his shoulder and it felt so comforting that I didn't care about the damn hymn."

P.P.S. 4:35 P.M.
Myra and I just got back from an invigorating walk through the bush right into Daisy's yard. The old place doesn't look too much different, asparagus fronds flowing in the autumn breeze, and then we strolled up the little knoll that leads past her magnificent enclosed swimming pool. You often commented on how wonderful it would be to float on your back in the warm blue water on winter days watching the snowflakes slowly fall through the trees from her floor to ceiling windows. The bush, itself, brought back so many happy memories of you and Myra and me, in the spring, and again in the fall, wandering around finding stone circles and derelict vehicles that continue to merge with the environment, creating their own art forms. Thanks for the memories, honey.

10 September 2013 — 9:43 A.M.

Darling,

On September 1, 2011, I wrote in my journal, "Boating all summer long with Myra and my favourite boyfriend. More time on the water than we've had in years. The other day we came down from the south end of the lake, cutting right down the middle. Lake was glassy, calm. Gulls flying overhead, swooping and soaring right along with us. Reminded me of another experience in the boat—a similar one with Drummer—a moment in time where things just stop, you take a mental picture, you never forget it."

XOX Martha

183

16 September—2:20 P.M.

Darling—

A glorious day to be in a tree house called Eden, the tall windows all open to the wind in the leaves (now turning golden) and then a tramp with Myra through the bush, past quaking aspens, silver birch, hazelnut bushes, along the ridge of trails that overlook Pelican Lake. A blue sky day, indeed. Maybe for the next little while I'll just gently and gratefully drift.

My dearest love,
Martha

30 September 2013

Darling Brian,

Looking across at the old tuberculosis sanatorium, where Dad and Mom made their living, I ponder the fact that healing is only available to the sick and/or weary when a place can be sunk into—or as you and I so often remarked, "sinking into it like a couple of stones."

My thought on this beautiful day is that we moved heaven and earth to have you here in the summer of 2012. I truly believe that your life was prolonged because of it. In removing the stress and noise and not so great air of the city we were able to concentrate on being rocked in the energy of this most natural setting. And while, ultimately, there was no cure for you, no pill to simply make your disease go away, you still were able to experience a beautiful stretch of time.

So it shouldn't be a revelation to me that here at Eden I've been doing my own "curing in the woods," and grief, though not an illness, can be assuaged by what those early tuberculosis patients were fortunate to be treated with—rest, good food, lack of stress, fresh air and an exquisite meditative view of the natural world. The time that remains here should shore me up well for the winter. My question, "Will you leave this beautiful place and come back to the city with me, my love?"

I love you,
Martha

Tuesday, 2 October 2013 — 11:27 A.M.

Darling,

On Sunday, briefly back in Winnipeg, I propped myself on Jeff's sofa as he sat across from me tinkering with the sound for our CD. The designer's concept for the cover is just in and we think it's fabulous; the artwork we chose—your photo of redwing blackbirds sitting in bare branches like musical notes against a blue sky and one other image that captures Pelican Lake in October—all set off with vibrant red.

As we listened to the music, I glanced out my jazz brother's window at yellow leaves and thought, again, about how lucky I am to have the shelter of art. I recalled how I was when we first started rehearsals—"wretched and bawling all the time"— to now as winter, spring, summer and fall have swept along and we have a CD that will be ready for sale by the end of the month and a release party planned soon after.

Through these many months, between the music and writing these letters to you, I've been able to live my life more fully than I would have without such beautiful distractions. And so, if I were to give advice to anyone who is sorrowing for their "dearly dead," it would be this: engage in the things you have always loved doing, whatever they may be. Even as they may be difficult to find the energy to do, you must somehow access them and use them as tools for digging out from under crushing loss. It also makes good sense if those distractions are in some way connected to the person you lost, because that gives meaning and purpose to the exercise.

185

I continue to be healed by Eden, the place we both loved so deeply, and it's good to reflect for another couple of weeks, but my personal work here feels done—that of getting my head on straight, finding solace in the curative power of nature, finding you everywhere I look, and continuing to find a way through art to stand as an only one—alone and no longer part of a very special couple.

Am I sad? Of course I am. Am I over it, have I moved past grief? Of course not. Another piece of advice I'd give to whomever needs it would be this: don't let anyone rush you through the process or make you feel somehow less because you are not "managing well." But do find someone to talk to; grief can be so isolating, and as my own wonderful counsellor, Karen, said early on in the process, "Everyone's grief is shaped differently."

Brian, you were a self-contained man, as I've said more than once in these love letters to you. You never changed yourself into some conveniently constructed plaster person for the occasion. Everyone you met, met the real you—and you were, quite literally, looked up to. What a legacy and what a tough act to follow. I may never, as you also wished for me, find "the boyfriend," but I'll know him if I see him. I'll walk into a room somewhere, as you and I did a lifetime ago, and he'll be the stranger who sets off a bell of deep recognition.

Meantime, for what remains of this, my first year of grieving, I'll continue to pour out my heart and mind to you on paper, keeping you alive in spirit, honouring your life. Who needs a headstone with a wife like me, right, darling?

All my love,
Martha

3 October 2013—8:44 A.M.

Brian honey, it's about five degrees above freezing and Myra and I have just returned from a little jaunt in the October woods where she found a "stick" that's about five feet long, maybe more. She somehow managed not to stab her eyes out when dashing through low face-slapping bushes in order to bring it home.

"My God," I said to her, "what a proud moment. That is just an amazing stick," as she pranced around the yard with it balanced between her teeth like a vaulting pole.

Called Gerry Paradis and we exchanged pleasantries about the cottage plumbing and the weather.

"No 'S' word in the forecast just yet," he said.

"Yes," I agreed, playfully adding, "No—shit! It's snow!—just yet."

He chuckled and instructed me to keep a tap running over-night if it got below freezing and stayed there, and I passed on the information that I'd be here at Eden until the weekend after Thanksgiving. Somebody from Paradise Plumbing will come by, as usual, and shut off the water.

No matter what the circumstances, it's always hard to leave this place, but as I said to Gerry, "See you next summer."

I love you,
Martha

11 October 2013—9:27 A.M.

Darling Brian,

As I sit here finishing my morning coffee, I am jogged by a memory—one that I've had sitting in the back of my mind to recall with you. Remember Iceland?

We were given an artist exchange there by the (Canadian)

Icelandic National League. I had a few speaking engagements—book talks and so on—but mostly we were going because I'd been offered a performance with the Reykjavik International Jazz Festival.

We'd hired some pretty amazing Toronto players—Dave Restivo, piano; Mike Downes, bass; Ted Warren, drums—all artists in their own right. Mike had that regular gig with jazz diva Molly Johnson, but as a unit I had a feeling that they'd really cook. (Later I found out that they'd all known each other since they were twelve.)

Before the Reykjavik Jazz Festival, however, our quartet was invited to perform as the season opener for a jazz series curated by a then unknown third cousin of mine, Jon Hlover Askelsson, up in Akureyri, in the north of Iceland.

Icelanders are such passionate genealogists. Neither you nor I ever were, and your cheeky comment, as an aside to me, usually went something like, "Your what is related to who?" Nonetheless, we were both charmed by the "cousins" who kept showing up, with intense enthusiasm, to gather us in during our stay—including my gentle beautiful third cousin Hanna Palsdottir, who told me with a twinkle, "Anyone who can't extract their connection from you will immediately claim you as their ninth cousin."

We were in Reykjavik a few days. We then took the flight up to Akureyri—a day and a half before my bandmates were due to arrive from Canada. It was November and snowing heavily, and we were met the airport by Jon. Two evenings later Dave and Mike and Ted and I opened his winter jazz series, Hot Thursdays at Deiglan, performing before a packed audience who cheered and whistled and asked for three encores.

"In Iceland," Jon, flushed with success, told us later, "it's considered an insult if the audience doesn't ask for at least one."

You and I went back to our hotel room that night feeling very confident about everything.

Next morning, after a late breakfast, we were all assembled in the lobby for the flight back to Reykjavik. Standing around, killing time, we were particularly taken with the way a bassist gets his instrument from one part of the world to another. A big stand-up bass, which is about six feet tall, fits into its regular hard case and then into a larger white travelling case that, it takes no imagination at all to think, resembles a coffin.

It was very windy that morning—November, we'd been told, is often a month of extremes. Jon had decided to take in our gig at the jazz festival, and as our own flight was filled, he'd booked an earlier one. Around eleven he called from the tarmac to say that, due to gale-force winds, no planes would be leaving Akureyri that day. Our return tickets, half used, would unfortunately not be refunded if we chose to make alternate plans. Our sound check was at six p.m. in Reykjavik, our performance slated for ten o'clock that evening. My musicians expected to perform, and as much as anything, be paid (well) by the Reykjavik Jazz Festival. The only solution Jon could see was to rent a taxi-van (at our expense) and speed from the north to the south—a trip of about four or five hours. If we decided to go that route it would take him awhile to make the necessary arrangements. You told him to go ahead.

Jon and the driver of the taxi-van arrived at the hotel around twelve-thirty. We loaded in, all eight of us (Ted had brought along his wife from Canada for a belated honeymoon) and I chose, as a good host, to sit with my cheek pressed against the window beside my seatmate, Mike's bass—the coffin.

Everything in Iceland is over-the top expensive and I figured the taxi-van would cost you and me around a thousand dollars Canadian, which it did. But as we all strapped in and I stuck my head over the bass to let everyone know what a good sport I was being, you turned from the front, winked, and told me with a mad grin, "I've always wanted to say, 'Driver, take me to Reykjavik!'"

We arrived at our venue in Reykjavik at two minutes to six. Later, we turned out a concert that Icelandic jazz festival–goers

189

embraced (two encores). And later still, as we all sat around the hotel, shooting the breeze before we turned in, Restivo and I decided to share a seventeen-dollar beer.

"You've earned it," you teased, as he and I rolled our eyes and meted out the beer into two small glasses. Outrageous price, especially in the year we were there, 2003, but nothing compared to the "taxi" ride.

Four months later, back at home, I got out of bed one shivery March morning and went to check my emails before going down to the kitchen to make coffee. There, on my computer, was an email from Berlin—inviting me not only to speak at the fourth International Literature Festival Berlin (all expenses paid), but would I also consider doing the festival wrap-up with an hour-long jazz concert?

I padded down the hall and snuggled back into bed with you. I think I may have been giggling.

You turned over and said, "What's up?"

"How would you like to go to Berlin in September?"

"When did this happen?"

"An email just now." Then I elaborated, adding the part about the jazz concert.

You smiled up at the ceiling, then back at me, "First we take Reykjavik—then we take Berlin."

Loving you, you bet,
Martha

# BOOK FOUR

# ALL MY TOMORROWS

"Not knowing when the dawn will come
I open every door."

— Emily Dickinson

1 November 2013—2:00 p.m.

Darling Brian,

Back in the old routine of city life. It's been a summer of separation for Kirsten and Mike and me. That's been a good thing, offering space and private healing time for us all. As a family unit, however, we're still healing, and living together continues to be a good arrangement.

The jazz brothers and I played a gig on Tuesday night and before that I had about twenty-four hours of dipping down into the old familiar chasm of grief. However, I pulled myself together and emerged to join them and we turned out a show for a packed audience—many of whom stayed for the last set, which went on until after eleven. On a Tuesday night that's late for most working people.

The CD, *All My Tomorrows* (named from the title track), looks beautiful, sounds beautiful (thanks to the magic of some pretty swell sound engineering on Jeff's part) and is selling well even before it's been launched.

This memoir is coming to fruition, too. But, Hello Brian—are you out there? I reach to grasp those otherworldly ethers of yours. I also keep forgetting that the minute I do, you slam back against my spirit in a kind of ghostly body check that says, "Yes? You called?" and the ferocity and beauty of you take my breath away. Oh yes, you keep taking care of business.

Your sister, Our Maureen, said in a phone call this morning, "It's incredible how far you've come, Martha, and how many amazing things have happened for you this year. It's as if he is and has been right with you."

"I know, and I'm not ready to let him go—not just yet."

"You don't have to—not ever, if you don't want to."

But cry, cry, cry, my dearest man. I want all six-foot-six of you standing behind me in a crowded room, your beautiful elegant hands resting along the tops of my shoulders. That would be so nice, so comforting.

My deepest love,
Martha


2 November 2013 — 9:34 A.M.

Darling,

I googled Brian Brooks this morning and came up with your obituary and, surprisingly, a number of other Brian Brooks's:

— A professor of journalism
— A choreographer
— A board member of an arts organization
— A professor of law
— A heroin pusher (for balance)
— A Brian Brooks whose face looked a lot like yours and who had also been the owner of a marketing and design company until, for the last seven years of his life, he was a ship's captain on the Great Lakes
— A Florida pediatrician
— A web designer
— A neuropsychologist
— A mental health therapist
— A photographer whose web gallery photo, entitled *Trees and Snow*, eerily resembles your photo (now on our living room wall) of *Trees and Round Hay Bales* in October, both shot in late fall, both shot in the mist, both with a definite feel of the French Impressionist painter Monet

So your namesakes inhabit their own little corners of the planet Earth, all making their own unique footprints, the thwarted uneasy life of the heroin pusher included.

I rest my case with all my love,
Martha

## Saturday 9 November 2013 — 8:37 A.M.

Darling Brian,

Almost a year without you. Coming to the end of writing this memoir, I've recently turned back to the novel I was working on earlier in the year, "Prose and Possibility." The manuscript, thus far, sparkles. I'm so happy to tell you that I'm still in love with our heroine, the tubercular Signy, her lovelorn column, her tenuous venturings at the age of twenty-two into the adult world of love, how she lives with the uncertainty of her life from a sanatorium bed and how she, indeed, makes a life and makes the world come to her.

There is much to be said for going away from a project for a while, doing something else, and then coming back with fresh eyes. This was something you always advised, in those everyday moments in our life when you'd come into my office as my head was bent over my work, massage the back of my neck and say, "Let's go for a walk now—you can come back to this later." Reluctantly I'd leave whatever I was working on, but then we'd be in the car going somewhere—often the tall-grass prairie section of Beaudry Park, that nature haven that's close to the city and close to our hearts. Once there, the dog—Drummy, and in later years, Myra—would bound ahead. If it was winter the yellow grasses would stick a couple of feet above the slumps of snow, and, bundled, we'd walk past them and talk, or not talk.

After an hour or two we'd come back to our warm house and I'd return to my office and you'd do whatever you did, house projects, cooking, reading, as the ghost of my novel once again opened brightly to my heart and mind and took me into its life, and my spirit would be fed by all that was so richly, for me, without and within.

I love you,
Martha

**Monday, 11 November 2013 — 8:51 A.M.**

Darling,

Two years ago today you were given a diagnosis that brought us to our knees and brought our normal life to a devastating halt. And yet, somehow, we managed to stand up again and go on with the help of so many people who loved us, our amazing daughter most ferociously among them.

And now I go on. I was talking to Jeff yesterday about CD stuff and he brought me up short with this surprising (to me) observation. He said, "There's no point to this life, life as a musician, unless you play like your life depended on it. Otherwise, why waste your time? I certainly don't want to go out and hear people unless they play that way."

"You sing that way," he went on. "Certainly in this past year that's the way you sing. As if your life depended on it. Which is why I work with you."

And so I go on and sing my life not for one now, darling, but for two. I know you're listening.

I love you,
Martha

**23 November 2013 — 8:24 A.M.**

My darling,

Have been fighting a cold, a bronchial/throat thing for about a week. Wish I felt better. So much is riding on tonight and the launch of *All My Tomorrows*. Ken and Pam Campbell, the couple hosting this event, are friends of Jeff and longtime patrons of the arts. They are accustomed to throwing fund-raising soirées for upwards of a hundred people—friends and associates in various forms of endeavour, law, government, medicine, broadcasting, the arts. They collect people like flowers and nurture them at their parties. We're expecting around seventy people—a collection of their own friends as well as Jeff's and mine.

Our Maureen sent a dozen roses that trail a beautiful scent, along with a note that reads, "Wish we could be there with you. Love, Maureen and Brian."

My longtime editor and friend, Shelley, sent an email at around six o'clock this morning, with the subject Star! and the message, "Will be thinking of you tonight. Have a great one! S xox"

A few weeks ago, feeling your hand steer me into a store on Corydon that sells beautiful clothing, some of it imported from Spain, I purchased a long form-fitting top in reds and oranges and deep purple that can only be described as wearable art. Tonight, I'll slip it over black tights and pull on some black boots and dangle a pair of honey amber earrings from my ears.

I'm going back to bed for a while. Kirsten, who also has "the plague" and is coughing her head off, told me, "It's not rocket science that you and I get sick right around this time, the anniversary of his death."

I've been ordered by everyone, including my producer, not to open my mouth until after I sing tonight.

All my love,
Your excited and/but sick Wife.


## 25 November 2013—8:48 A.M.

My darling Brian,

The LeBlancs, Deb and Marv, drove in from Ninette for this shindig, bringing a whole pack of summer memories with them as they came in the door. Their store, The Grocery Box, and everyone who works there provides centring in the day for lots of lonely people, and this summer your grieving wife was among them. Marv's first wife, as you recall, died of brain cancer, and he and Deb and I will forever be connected by that powerful detail. "It's a challenging journey, isn't it," Marv said to me, a little teary, one day in the summer of 2012 as you and I were leaving the store.

Anyway, Saturday night they arrived in their party togs with throngs of other people, all a tangle of scarves and mitts and coats and boots, the crisp winter night swirling out into the darkness behind them. Deb handed me flowers—not just any kind of flowers, but, when I unwrapped them, an over-the-top bouquet of two dozen roses, one dozen red, one dozen white. I felt like an opera diva. Kate, who'd been chaperoning me so I wouldn't talk until I sang, went dashing through the crowd to the kitchen to find a vase. Canapes were coming out of the oven. Bottles of wine kept appearing with the celebrants and soon covered one entire table. Kirsten, looking like a flamenco dancer, and Mike like a young Tolstoy, set up a CD table in a corner adjacent to Ken and Pam's grand piano.

In an aside to me Deb, somewhat awestruck, said, "I've never seen a grand piano right in the middle of somebody's living room before."

Steve and Rob arrived with their instruments. I stood around holding up big tall Steve's big tall bass, as has been our custom on gigs for the past seventeen years, while he disappeared to find someplace to lay the case. Rob quietly and deftly went about setting up his drum kit—which says a lot about how he plays—you were always talking about his beautiful brush work, honey. Jeff and I had arrived earlier with our gear and he was now running a cord in front of the piano, connecting my mic to his spanking-new sound system—which is German-made (Bose, you'd love it) and makes him deeply happy.

Ken and Pam's house has two interconnected living rooms, and as more people arrived they spread out, chatting volubly, carrying glasses of wine. Some sat or stood all down the staircase that overlooked the piano so they could see the action. Others milled in the kitchen or dining room or wandered off to comfy couches near the fireplace. I introduced Deb to our dear friend Sharon Jasper and they discovered, to their mutual joy, that they are related. Walter

Isaac, a healing practitioner and member of Jeff's Finnegan's Wake Book Club, beckoned me to cozy up on a couch beside him where he could do some energy work on me.

"You're feeling pretty good," he said after a bit. "You ready for this?"

"Yep. If my voice holds out."

"It will," he said with a sweet smile, stroking his hand along my back.

That was the evening's first visitation from you.

Jeff and Rob and Steve got things underway by playing their own set. It was full of life and distracting beauty. I couldn't wait to wrap my hands around my mic and join them.

I frequented the CD table and wordlessly signed CDs as Kirsten and Mike did a brisk business from that grey metal cash box you set up so nicely for my book launch at Ninette in 2010.

After about half an hour Katie and I went upstairs and I hauled a bottle of cognac out of my music bag. ("Good," my producer had said to me earlier. "It'll warm your throat and loosen you up a bit.")

Three Christmases ago, if you'll remember, Brian, you gave me that bottle. I knew I was saving the tail ends of it for a good reason.

"Spirits from the spirit," I giggled to Katie as I poured about an inch and a half into the small brandy snifter I'd also brought along.

We returned downstairs where Kirsten, spying the glass in my hand, said, "That's great, Mom—but sip it slowly and remember you're sick and you haven't eaten much today."

"Right," I said. "I promise it'll be a slow burn, honey."

It was. Right from the opening of what Jeff and I refer to as the salacious and wonderful "Teach Me Tonight," to our out-there smoky take on "Bei Mir Bist Du Schon," to "All My Tomorrows," "The Second Time Around," "Call Me Irresponsible," "It's You or No One," "The Things We did Last Summer," "It's Been a Long Long Time," "All the Way," "Day by Day," my voice and the music of my sweet jazz brothers soared up to you and back to the gathering and out again, the deep holy profane beautiful soul of song connecting all of us.

Between songs I talked about how the idea for the CD began with one song, "All the Way," back in January and about Jeff's part in all of this. I was also able, without crying, to talk about you. I said, among other things, "Brian was six-foot-six and the handsomest men I ever laid eyes on." I told them how we met. I introduced everyone to Kirsten and Kate and to "Brian's best friend," Nancy, who was sitting on the floor right across from me.

After we finished the set, Nancy said, "I have the strongest feeling Brian's here tonight. While you were singing he was standing directly behind you."

"He wouldn't miss this for the world," I told her.

(You behind me, your hands resting on my shoulders.)

"He's wearing a rich-coloured brown shirt with small bright beige checks," she went on.

"I believe you. He often wore that in the winter to my jazz gigs."

Kirsten saw you superimposed on a very tall man. Kate saw you drifting quite literally through the crowd. Margaret MacKinnon said you were there. Maureen Hunter, too, strongly sensed your presence. And I felt you surrounding me all evening, with all your strength and chest-popping pride.

After singing, when I was finally able to talk to people, the woman whose husband Kirsten saw you superimposed on came up to me with him in tow. They were both beaming and said, "I want you to meet my husband. He's almost six-foot-six."

Another woman with tears in her eyes hugged and kissed me, and thanked me for introducing you to everyone and for "risking being vulnerable." Then she said, "You were so lucky to have had a love with him like that, it's rare."

After the music and a rush of CD sales, Jeff and I found a quiet corner of a couch to squeeze in together while balancing plates of food on our laps. "You were doing some things with your voice tonight that were unique," he said. "Your timing was off the map. I kept saying to myself, 'where is she taking this?' and then you'd take it somewhere that was unexpected and completely appropriate."

What can I say about Jeff, one of the best jazz teachers I've ever worked with—friend, producer, arranger, pianist, sound engineer, therapist, and, as I've been telling him lately, one-man band-aid.

At one in the morning, after I'd had a couple of glasses of wine, Mike, another one-man band-aid, said, "I'm driving you home."

An email from Jeffrey in Toronto was waiting for me when we got back. He'd been fretting and wanted me to tell him before I went to bed that it had been a great success—so I did.

He called on Sunday and I told him, "I don't know why it all worked so well. I shouldn't even have had a voice."

"I do," said our friend. "It worked because you are an amazing woman, Martha. Through music you found a way out of the darkness. It's an external balm to heal wounds that are soul deep and you're using that pain to deliver a message of courage and hope. That's what people are connecting with."

But it's you who are amazing, honey. It was all part of your plan, wasn't it. Your hand has been all over these merciful miracles that have sprung up like beautiful flowers, all of this transforming, sad and surprising past year.

Amen my darling,
Martha


### Wednesday, 27 November 2013—10:24 A.M.

Hello darling,

Well, we've made it through the first year. I'm no less in love with you at the end of it all than I was at the beginning. And my writing hand hurts—sore-ow. I'm in bed today with what my doctor is calling "a viral bronchitis"—I made it through the CD launch and then fell apart. So be it, it was all worth it.

This grieving process is tough work, but "hello" all of you out there who are reading this and slowly marking off your own anniversaries of loss. I'm here to confer with you about this pain—about how, after a year, it doesn't pull you under quite so profoundly as it did at the first when you were being dragged to the bottom of the ocean, lost, alone, and hoping be rescued.

And so, Brian, honey, I keep calling you in—even when I'm not aware that I'm doing so. Yesterday I had a treatment with my massage therapist, Lindsay. As I lay on my stomach and she worked on my left leg, I drifted and gave myself up to her tender care. At first I was aware only of her hands, the long pull on my muscles, the gentle rhythm. Gradually, though, I noticed that there weren't only her hands working on my leg. There were three. Couldn't be three, I thought. But no, absolutely there were three. A larger hand with long elegant warm fingers had joined Lindsay's smaller ones. It was your unmistakable touch. You and she worked on my leg for four or five minutes. How wonderful to feel your touch again! And then, when she switched over to the other leg, it was just her again, and at this point I mentioned it.

"Oh, I just love my job," she said. "I just love it when that happens."

There are those, of course, who would sign in with their opinions, deftly explaining away what happened. To them I say, please allow me the comfort of this new miracle and keep your opinions to yourself. Grief is complex, God is complex, love is complex. All of it moves through us and shifts and dances as surely as do the ephemeral but brilliant northern lights. I take you in, Brian, and release you, and take you back in again. You move inside every breath I take, inside every beat of my heart.

## LATER—3:45 P.M.

Just back from a fine session with Karen Toole. I told her about my experience with your hand yesterday.

"First of all," she told me, "you are not hallucinating. Brian was there in the room. It was him. I tell people when they have experiences like that, 'believe it, you are coming into the holy of the moment.' But many of them will still clam up with others anyway—their experience devalued one way or another—and so they won't talk about it again. But people tell me these things over and over in my practice. As you and I have discussed, the veil is thin between this world and the next."

She went on, "Brian will never leave you, Martha. All the experiences you've had in this past year held up a mirror to you. Some would have looked away. But you looked right into the face of grief and you never looked away. These letters to Brian will show others what it's like to look so closely, and that it's a good and helpful thing to do."

I showed her the video of the stills of our life together that we played at your funeral. "My God," she said, when she saw our wedding picture, "he looks so strong. I've counselled a lot of young couples over the years and the guys, for the most part, look terrified. But just look at him," she chuckled. "He looks like he's all fired up and saying, 'Let's go!'"

We talked again of Karen's own dead, "my dead," as she calls them. She told me she once gave a talk on grief at the Marlborough Hotel. Beforehand she was sitting, preparing her notes, in a little restaurant near the lobby, as more and more people kept streaming in from the night.

"I thought to myself, I hope to God they aren't all coming to hear me. What makes me think I'm an authority on this? And then the answer came, 'my dead have given me the credentials— my mother, my father, my brother, my sister.' When I finally got up to talk I threw out everything I'd prepared. I stood before a crowd of 800 people and the first thing I said was, 'When you see me standing up here, you aren't looking at a woman alone, there are five of us.' I felt the room warm up. I felt my dear dead mother's arms come around me, holding me up. I don't remember what I said after that. I just remember how I began the whole thing. How powerful that was."

I had been telling her, Brian, that one of the things that kills me about you not being around anymore is that people will never know how special you were and what a special couple we were.

"But you see," said Karen, "anytime anyone looks at you, they'll see him, too. He's part of you. He's right there holding you up, supporting you, and that's never going to change. Believe in it. Believe in him and what he still can do for you."

And so, my darling, I'll close off this letter to you and think about the value of this woman's advice, of how she has valued my journey and valued getting to know you.

She asked what I thought the next year would bring.

"You've been going pretty hard on your creative work," she said. "So what's going to pull you through this next leg of your journey?"

"Writing and music," I said. "Now and always."

"Well, Brian couldn't be more pleased," she told me. "He wanted you to live your life and you're doing it."

I keep looking into the darkness, honey, looking for ways to find the light, and there you are, tall and handsome and meltingly supportive, beckoning me on.

All my love,
Martha

## Acknowledgements:

There are a great many people to thank—friends and family and others—who lifted me up in the first shattering year of Brian's absence from our lives. I reached out and they reached right back. They are my tribe and my gratitude runs deep and endless.

Thanks, most especially, to my daughter Kirsten and son-in-law Mike, who held me in their mighty embrace and refused to let go even as sorrow washed all three of us to the bottom of the sea of grief.

My sister, Alice, and brother-in-law, Eddie, who provided a couch, a warm meal and a glass of lovely red wine every Saturday night—as well as a blanket to cover me when I was cold and a never-ending supply of Kleenex.

My dear jazz brother, Jeff Presslaff, for his unwavering affection, friendship and music therapy. He truly is a one-man bandaid.

My deep-hearted grief counsellor, Karen Toole, whose wise advice is sprinkled liberally throughout. If I didn't always capture her exact words, her intent and message is unassailable: Stay true to the face of grief and do not look away.

To Patricia Barber, for her words which I have exactly quoted, and for the unexpected joy of her hand-in-friendship. How pleased Brian would be and how utterly amazed!

And there are so many wonderful others, only a fraction of whom I will name here: Pauline and Rodney (Wood/Steiman), Sharon and Darvin Jasper, Maureen Hunter, Marilyn Hokanson, Pat Farrell, Maureen Brooks, Daryl and Allan Brooks, Deb and Marv LeBlanc, Shelley Tanaka, Jeffrey Canton, Kate McDonald, Aaron Hughes, Vincent Champagne, Nancy Gilbert, Agnes Comack, Michelle Grégoire, Margaret and Brian MacKinnon.

Thanks to the team at Turnstone Press, Jamis Paulson, Sharon Caseburg, and Michelle Palansky, who made my "homecoming" to a Winnipeg publishing house so joyful and lush and "right down the street!" And as well my editor, Catherine Marjoribanks, for her discerning and elegant eye, and Heidi Harms for judicious tweaking.

The Manitoba Arts Council provided generous financial support during the writing of *Letters to Brian* and I am, as always, deeply grateful to them.

Epigraphs and quotes by Patricia Barber, Miles Davis, and Karen Toole are used with permission. The quote by Edward Livingston Trudeau on page 176 is from his presidential address at the Eighth Congress of American Physicians and Surgeons in Washington, 1910.